Contents

About Viva!

Viva! is a vivacious campaigning charity. We work on all vegan issues and investigate how the big names farm and kill animals. One of our long running campaigns, *White Lies*, researched the health impact of dairy on our health. Another, *Scary Dairy*, shows how dairy cows and calves are treated by the major players in the industry. It also has fantastic info on going dairy-free. See scarydairy.org.uk

Viva! publishes the highly acclaimed *Viva!life* magazine and runs the popular online Vegan Recipe Club veganrecipeclub.org.uk. Viva! also loves helping people to take the step to a healthy, humane diet and so has wonderful, inspirational but, most of all, useful resources, including viva.org.uk/easyvegan

About Viva! Health

Our experts research and campaign for healthy vegan diets. There is a really helpful website viva.org.uk/health which includes the *A-Z of Nutrients* and *A-Z of Diseases*. There are also great sections on vegan diets for sports people and for all stages of life – including children, the mature and during pregnancy. It's all here!

Vegan for the Planet
Why vegan diets are best for wildlife, the environment and the future
By Dr Justine Butler, Viva! with additional research by Jasmine Clark, BSc, MSc, Viva!
© Viva! 2023

Produced by: Viva!, 8 York Court, Wilder St, Bristol BS2 8QH
T: 0117 944 1000 (Mon-Fri 9am-5pm)
E: info@viva.org.uk
W: viva.org.uk
Registered charity 1037486

Introduction

The planet is in trouble, global temperatures and sea levels are rising, air pollution is choking us, water is running out and deserts are spreading into areas where life once thrived. Chemicals running off farmland into estuaries and coastal waters (eutrophication) are leading to aquatic dead zones. Rainforests are being torn down and oceans decimated. Precious areas of wilderness around the world are being squeezed and we are living through the world's sixth mass extinction with one million species living under threat.

One single industry lies at the heart of all this destruction – not one we must rely on, but one many people choose to support – animal agriculture. The production of meat, fish, eggs and dairy is a main driver of all these environmental issues and simply changing your diet could make all the difference.

Many of us are trying to reduce our carbon footprint by flying less, walking and cycling more, recycling and reducing food waste. But the cow in the room is our food system – the Government has consistently failed to acknowledge the devastating role animal agriculture has on the planet.

Our food choices lie at the heart of tackling the climate crisis, reducing water stress

A VEGAN DIET IS PROBABLY THE SINGLE BIGGEST WAY TO REDUCE YOUR IMPACT ON PLANET EARTH

and pollution, restoring land back to forest or grassland, and protecting the world's wildlife. Environmental researcher from the University of Oxford, Joseph Poore, says: "A vegan diet is probably the single biggest way to reduce your impact on planet Earth, not just greenhouse gases, but global acidification, eutrophication, land use and water use" (Carrington, 2018).

Climate crisis

If we carry on with business as usual, tearing down forests, expanding animal agriculture and increasing the levels of greenhouse gases in the atmosphere, we can expect more of the following:

- Many plants and animals will become extinct
- The loss of wildlife will increase, threatening important ecosystems
- Ocean acidification will destroy marine life
- Glaciers and sea ice will melt
- Sea levels will rise
- Coastal cities will flood
- Places that currently get lots of rain and snowfall will get hotter and drier
- Lakes and rivers will dry up
- Droughts will make it hard to grow crops
- There will be water shortages
- Less predictable seasons will threaten food security
- Hurricanes, tornadoes and storms will become more common
- Certain diseases will increase, eg malaria and dengue fever
- The likelihood of conflict will increase

Source: EKOenergy, 2020.

As a result of climate change, we are now seeing extreme weather events more frequently around the world. During the summer of 2022, intense heatwaves covered large swathes of Europe, China and North America. Temperature records were broken in the UK, Italy, France, Switzerland, Germany, Poland, Hungary and Slovenia and there were 24,000 heat-related deaths in Europe alone. According to the World Weather Attribution group, climate change made the record drought across the northern hemisphere at least 20 times more likely. Without it, they say, such an event would happen only once every 400 years (WWA, 2022).

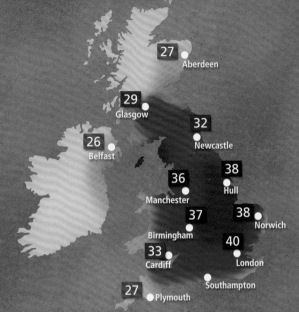

Figure 1. Record-breaking high temperatures across the UK during the European heatwave in 2022

Source: World Meteorological Organisation, 2022.

During these heatwaves, many places across the UK – with records dating back over 100 years – recorded their highest ever temperature. As shown in Figure 1, temperatures exceeded 40°C for the first time in recorded history. There was little respite at night as records were set then too, for example, Kenley Airfield in Greater London recorded a new highest minimum (night-time) temperature of 25.8°C (Met Office, 2022).

The UK Met Office issued its first ever red warning for heat, while the UK Health Security Agency issued its first level 4 heat-health alert and the Government declared a national emergency. A red warning means adverse health effects are expected, not just to those most vulnerable. The intense heat affected the entire nation, driving a rise in hospitalisations, triggering widespread fires and causing severe disruption to transport.

In August 2022, the Government of Pakistan also declared a national emergency but for a very different reason. Unprecedented rainfall from mid-June until the end of August left a third of the country under water. The rains and flooding affected over 33 million people, destroyed 1.7 million homes and nearly 1,500 people died. Again, the World Weather Attribution group assessed how climate change had impacted this extreme weather event and found that it could have increased the most intense rainfall over a short period in the worst affected areas by 50 per cent (WWA, 2022a).

These are just a few examples, there will be more to come as the IPCC warn that as much as 40 per cent of the world's population, a staggering 3.5 billion people, are highly vulnerable to climate impacts (IPCC, 2022). It sounds as terrifying as a science fiction disaster movie but it's not unrealistic. The 2015 film *Mad Max: Fury Road* is set in a desolate barren wasteland where water is scarce and becomes a lot scarier when you realise this is where we are headed. NASA's

3.5 BILLION PEOPLE ARE HIGHLY VULNERABLE TO CLIMATE IMPACTS

senior water scientist, Dr James Famiglietti, says: "There are metaphorical elements of *Mad Max* that are already happening, and that will only worsen with time" (Howard, 2016).

It is not just mass extinctions and extreme weather events we need to be concerned about (as if that wasn't bad enough), but also political unrest, mass migrations and conflict. Future wars being fought over water are becoming a real possibility. The future of the planet is at stake and urgent action is needed now.

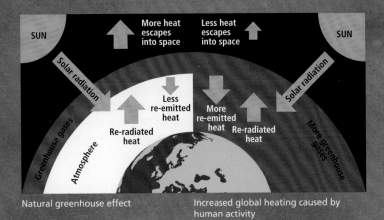

Natural greenhouse effect

Increased global heating caused by human activity

Figure 2. The greenhouse effect

Global heating

As shown in Figure 2, the Earth is surrounded by a layer of gases we call the atmosphere. It forms a protective layer, protecting us from the sun's harmful rays and preventing extreme temperature changes. However, as the gases build up, they act like the glass that greenhouses are made from – letting sunlight in and trapping the heat. Human activity, such as animal agriculture, has increased the amount of gases in the atmosphere and global temperatures are rising.

Carbon dioxide (CO_2) is the most abundant greenhouse gas and is now 50 per cent higher than in 1750 – the beginning of industrial times (Carbon Brief, 2021). Other gases, such as methane and nitrous oxide, are emitted in smaller quantities but trap heat more effectively and can be many times stronger.

How animal agriculture contributes to emissions

Animal agriculture contributes 20 per cent of all greenhouse gas emissions, including animal feed crop production (Xu et al., 2021). In 2006, the United Nations' report *Livestock's Long Shadow* estimated that livestock farming accounted for 18 per cent of man-made greenhouse gas emissions – a bit lower but still more than all the world's transport – cars, buses, trucks, trains, ships and planes – combined (FAO, 2006). In 2013, the Food and Agriculture Organisation of the United Nations (FAO) revised the figure lower still to 14.5 per cent (Gerber et al., 2013). However, scientists say this estimate was based on outdated data, and livestock emissions, especially methane, are likely to be much higher because breeding and feeding methods have changed (BMC, 2017; Twine, 2021).

ANIMAL AGRICULTURE CONTRIBUTES A FIFTH OF ALL GREENHOUSE GAS EMISSIONS

The meat industry likes to distort statistics in their favour and talks about livestock's 'direct' emissions being closer to 10 per cent (rather than 20 per cent), ignoring land use changes such as deforestation. This is an unacceptable deception. The leading drivers of deforestation are expanding pastures for beef and soya, to feed poultry, pigs and other livestock including farmed fish. Around 80 per cent of global soya is used for animal feed, while just seven per cent of it is used for foods for direct human consumption, such as tofu and soya milk. In the UK, and many other countries, the vast majority of farmed animals are raised in factory farms and fed animal feed crops, such as soya, rather than roaming around fields munching grass all day. It's not a pretty picture, it involves extreme cruelty and the environmental impacts are devastating.

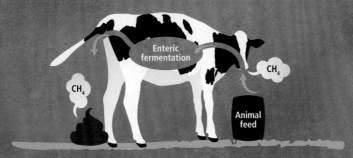

Figure 3. The production of methane from enteric fermentation in ruminant animals

Methane (CH_4)

Animal agriculture is the main source of the potent greenhouse gas methane, with large amounts coming from cows, sheep, goats, deer and antelope. These animals are called ruminants – hoofed grazing herbivores that get nutrients from plant foods by fermenting them in a specialised stomach with four compartments that helps them breakdown tough, fibrous plant matter. This process is called enteric fermentation (see Figure 3) and it produces large amounts of methane gas which exit the animal – mostly in their burps rather than their farts. Substantial amounts of methane also come from rotting liquid manure stored in ponds, tanks and outdoor earth-banked basins called manure lagoons. Other sources include forest fires, often where trees are being cleared for grazing or animal feed crops.

Research from the Institute for Agriculture and Trade Policy and Changing Markets Foundation (IATP) found that 15 of the world's biggest meat and dairy companies emit more methane than countries such as Russia, Canada, Australia or Germany. They found that the emissions from five meat and 10 dairy corporations were equal to more than 80 per cent of the European Union's total methane footprint and accounted for 11 per cent of the entire world's livestock-related methane emissions (IATP, 2022). Writing in the *Guardian*, Shefali Sharma, director of the IATP's European office said:

"That just blew my mind. We can't continue to have this handful of companies controlling this many animals" (Krupnick, 2022). The IATP's report calls for more ambitious action to cut emissions from the meat and dairy sector.

Methane can have a big effect on the climate because it has more than 80 times the warming power of carbon dioxide over the first 20 years after it reaches the atmosphere. Concentrations in the atmosphere have more than doubled since the industrial revolution (IPCC, 2021) and scientific research estimates that 25 per cent of today's warming is driven by methane from human activities (GOV.UK, 2022), making it an ideal target for mitigating climate change.

Reducing methane emissions is one of the most effective ways to rapidly reduce warming and could significantly help global efforts to limit temperature rise to 1.5°C. If methane emissions were cut by 45 per cent by 2030 this could avoid nearly 0.3°C of global heating by the 2040s. It would also, each year, prevent 255,000 premature deaths, 775,000 asthma-related hospital visits, 73 billion hours of lost labour from extreme heat and 26 million tonnes of crop losses globally (UNEP and Climate and Clean Air Coalition, 2021).

Carbon dioxide (CO_2)

Trees are an important carbon sink – meaning that they take carbon from the atmosphere and store it overground in their trunks and branches and underground in their roots. When trees are cut down and burned to make way for livestock grazing or growing crops for animal feed, carbon is released and carbon dioxide levels in the atmosphere increase. It gets worse, the damage grazing animals then cause to deforested land results in soil erosion, which releases more carbon and can lead to flooding.

Nitrous oxide (N_2O)

Nitrous oxide is commonly known as laughing gas but is almost 300 times as potent as carbon dioxide at heating the atmosphere, which is not so funny! Agriculture is also the main contributor of this greenhouse gas with nitrogen fertilisers being the primary source. Fertiliser is used extensively in crop production and as over a third of the world's cereal crop is fed to animals, it follows that animal agriculture is a huge and unnecessary source of this potent gas.

The beef with beef

Animal-based foods are an inefficient and wasteful use of precious resources. Beef is one of the most wasteful and damaging industries globally, producing 40 to 60 per cent of animal agriculture's emissions (Gerber *et al.*, 2013; FAO, 2022). It's responsible for vast losses of carbon sinks in land use changes, deforestation, biodiversity loss, excessive water wastage and pollution.

Much of the food cows eat is used in metabolism (normal body functions), building inedible body parts (bones, hooves, hair etc) and excreted. This is why it takes around 100 times as much land to produce a calorie of beef than it does to produce a calorie of plant-based alternatives. The same is true for protein – it takes almost 100 times as much land to produce a gram of protein from beef compared to tofu (Poore and Nemecek, 2018).

The production of beef and dairy foods produces substantially more greenhouse gas emissions than pig meat, chicken or eggs. While methane is a significant contributor, it is not the only reason for the large emissions of beef and dairy. Livestock grazing and the production of animal feed crops are the main driver of global deforestation and land use change – huge contributors of greenhouse gases. Other sources include managing pastureland (fertilisers and irrigation), nitrous oxide from manure, energy used by machinery, equipment and transport of cows to slaughter, plus food waste, which can be high for meat. Even if you discount methane entirely, foods produced from ruminants still have a high carbon footprint; the average footprint of beef, excluding methane, is still 10 to 100 times the footprint of most plant-based foods (Poore and Nemecek, 2018).

But humans can't eat grass so why not use land we can't grow wheat or potatoes on, for example, for grazing? The idea that marginal land, with low agricultural value, can't be used for anything other than grazing animals is simply wrong. Hardy human-edible plants, such as leafy greens, roots, buckwheat, rye, barley, quinoa and

leguminous plants (beans and other pulses) can all grow in a wide variety of conditions. In fact, growing plants improves soil health and reduces soil compaction that results from years of grazing animals stamping down the earth. Furthermore, fruit and nut trees could also be grown on rough and marginal lands to supplement these vegetable and cereal crops.

A largescale shift to a vegan diet would reduce the total amount of land we use for agriculture by a whopping 75 per cent – an area the size of North America, plus Brazil. This vegan shift would free up all grazing land with huge benefits for biodiversity and carbon storage as well as providing the opportunity for growing more plant foods. Other land could go back to rough grasslands, supporting multiple grasses, wildflower species and the wild animals that occupy these habitats. There would be an overall massive reduction in land use and we would be able to produce enough food to feed everyone in the world a nutritious diet. But this would only be possible with a widespread shift towards a vegan diet.

Dairy disaster

Dairy produces around 20 per cent of livestock's emissions – more than pig meat, poultry and eggs combined (Gerber *et al.*, 2013). In the EU, dairy produces more emissions than beef (Lesschen *et al.*, 2011). Globally, the dairy industry produces four per cent of greenhouse gas emissions (Gerber *et al.*, 2010). This is a significant amount – especially when you consider that over 70 per cent of the world's population is lactose intolerant and doesn't consume any dairy products.

Writing in the *Lancet*, public health researcher Professor Anthony J. McMichael said: "For the world's higher-income populations, greenhouse gas emissions from livestock farming warrant the same scrutiny as those from driving and flying" (McMichael *et al.*, 2007).

Founder of FAIRR and chief investment officer at Coller Capital, Jeremy Coller, says: "In

COWS ARE THE NEW COAL

stark contrast to the transport sector, only one in four meat, fish and dairy producers even measure their greenhouse gas emissions, let alone act to reduce them. The Paris Agreement is impossible to achieve without tackling factory farm emissions. Coal is a stranded asset, and cows are the new coal."

We are used to seeing the calorie content of food on product packaging and restaurant menus. If foods also carried a carbon label, showing their impact on the environment, people would have more opportunity to reduce their food-related footprint. Viva!'s *Eating the Earth* campaign is calling on the Government to make it a legal requirement for all UK restaurants to include the carbon footprint of food offered on their menus. See viva.org.uk/eating-the-earth

The meat industry says it's unrealistic to expect people to stop eating meat, but scientists say it is entirely possible to imagine a future world in which the consumption of meat is rare. We need to challenge these barriers, lift the lid on these industries and put changing diet at the top of the climate agenda.

The carbon footprint of food

The carbon footprint of food is a measure of all the greenhouse gases relating to the production of that food or meal. So, it includes growing, farming, processing, transporting, storing, cooking and disposing of food.

The carbon footprint of meat, fish, dairy and eggs is considerably higher than that of virtually all plant foods – with beef topping the list. In an average European diet, meat and eggs alone account for more than half (56 per cent) of all the food-related greenhouse gases emitted (Sandström *et al.*, 2018). Table 1 shows how vegan meals tend to produce considerably lower emissions than animal-based meals. A roast dinner made with beef, for example, produces 8.67 kilograms of CO_2-equivalents, whereas a nut roast produces just 0.3 kilograms – significantly lower!

In 2018, the most comprehensive analysis to date of the damage animal agriculture does to the planet was published in the journal *Science*. In the landmark study involving almost 40,000 farms in 119 countries, the environmental impacts of 40 food products that

Table 1. The carbon emissions of a selection of meat-based meals compared to vegan alternatives

Meat-based meals			Vegan meal alternatives		
Beef burger	E	3.05 kg CO_2e	Vegan burger	A	0.27 kg CO_2e
Beef roast dinner	E	8.67 kg CO_2e	Nut roast dinner	A	0.3 kg CO_2e
Lasagne	E	4.18 kg CO_2e	Lentil lasagne	A	0.3 kg CO_2e
Spaghetti bolognese	E	4.28 kg CO_2e	Lentil bolognese	A	0.31 kg CO_2e
Chicken korma	D	1.18 kg CO_2e	Quorn korma	B	0.43 kg CO_2e
Lamb kebab	E	2.08 kg CO_2e	Falafel wrap	B	0.25 kg CO_2e
Steak pie	E	7.33 kg CO_2e	Vegan pie	A	0.18 kg CO_2e
Toad in the hole	E	2.27 kg CO_2e	Vegan toad in the hole	B	0.34 kg CO_2e
Bangers & mash	C	1.71 kg CO_2e	Vegan bangers & mash	A	0.72 kg CO_2e
English fry up	D	3.12 kg CO_2e	Vegan fry up	B	1.38 kg CO_2e

Source: All carbon calculations provided in this table are an estimate using My Emissions Food Carbon Footprint Calculator: https://myemissions.green/food-carbon-footprint-calculator. Products/meals are rated from A (very low) to E (very high).

represent 90 per cent of all that is eaten were assessed. It looked at impacts from farm to fork, on land use, climate change emissions, freshwater use, water pollution (eutrophication) and air pollution (acidification). It compared beef with peas, for example, and found that producing one kilogram of beef emits almost 100 kilograms of greenhouse gases, whereas one kilogram of peas emits just one kilogram of gases (Poore and Nemecek, 2018).

Another study compared beef to soya and found that one kilogram of beef creates the same amount of emissions as driving 100 miles in a car, while soya produces the same as driving just three miles (Carlsson-Kanyama and González, 2009).

Lamb emits nearly 40 kilograms of gases per kilogram, and cheese, over 20. Pork and chicken have lower footprints (10-12 kilograms) but

100 miles

3 miles

What are CO_2-equivalents?

Because not all greenhouse gases are the same, carbon dioxide equivalents or 'CO_2e' is a way of describing the global warming potential of different greenhouse gases in a common unit. The idea is to express the impact of any given gas in terms of how much carbon dioxide would produce the same amount of warming. Methane, for example, is 80 times more powerful than carbon dioxide at warming the Earth over 20 years. Nitrous oxide is almost 300 times more potent.

Source: IPCC, 2021.

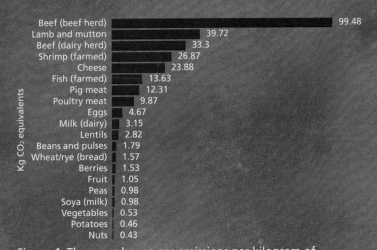

Figure 4. The greenhouse gas emissions per kilogram of different foods

Source: Poore and Nemecek, 2018.

are still higher than most plant-based foods. Lentils and tofu emit around three kilograms and most other beans and pulses, less than two.

If you look at the emissions from different food products in Figure 4, you will see how beef tops the table followed by other animal products, with plant-based foods producing the least.

Dairy versus plant-based milk

Cow's milk and dairy products are a staple in many people's diets but make a substantial contribution to the greenhouse gas emissions of food. In typical European diets, dairy accounts for over a quarter of the carbon footprint, sometimes exceeding a third (Sandström *et al.*, 2018).

Dairy alternatives have now become a mainstream choice with one in every three people in the UK opting for plant-based milks – and almost half of 25 to 44-year-olds. This is good news for the planet as all plant milks (eg soya, rice, oat and almond), have a much lower environmental impact than dairy.

	Greenhouse gas emissions (kg CO₂e)	Land use (m2)	Water use (L)
Cow's milk	3.2	9.0	628
Rice milk	1.2	0.3	270
Soya milk	1.0	0.7	28
Oat milk	0.9	0.8	48
Almond milk	0.7	0.5	371

Figure 5. The environmental impacts of dairy and plant-based milks

Source: Poore and Nemecek, 2018.

Figure 5 shows how, in all aspects, cow's milk has significantly higher environmental impacts than plant-based milks. Cow's milk produces around three times more greenhouse gas emissions, uses around 10 times as much land and two to 20 times as much freshwater. If you want to reduce the environmental impacts of your diet, switching to plant-based milk is a great place to start.

If the world is to meet its climate targets and strive for the optimistic target of 1.5°C, big dietary changes will be necessary. While increasing agricultural efficiency, reducing waste, limiting excess consumption, increasing yields and reducing the emission intensity of livestock production might reduce food-related emissions to a degree, they would not have the same impact as a global transition to a vegan diet (Eisen and Brown, 2022). A vegan diet could halve your food emissions (Scarborough *et al.*, 2014).

Land use

About 70 per cent of the Earth's surface is covered with water and the remaining 30 per cent is land. Not all of this land is habitable; nearly a fifth of it is described as 'barren land' (including deserts, salt flats, exposed rocks, beaches and sand dunes) and 10 per cent is made up of glaciers – the majority in Antarctica (World Economic Forum, 2022). This leaves what we call 'habitable land'. People have been changing and reshaping the world's habitable land for thousands of years, clearing forests and grasslands to grow crops and graze livestock.

Figure 6 shows how ten thousand years ago, 99 per cent of the world's habitable land was either forest or grassland – the remaining one per cent was taken up by freshwater rivers and lakes. Since then, humans have cleared two-thirds of wild grasslands and one-third of the world's forests. These have been replaced with cropland and grazing land (World Economic Forum, 2022). This change of land use has come at a huge cost to the planet's biodiversity and lies at the heart of the climate crisis.

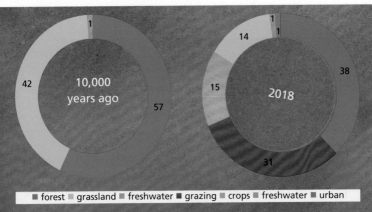

■ forest ■ grassland ■ freshwater ■ grazing ■ crops ■ freshwater ■ urban

Figure 6. Land use changes and forest loss over the last 10,000 years

Source: World Economic Forum, 2022.

One of the main reasons why animal agriculture is such a disproportionately wasteful use of land is because of the inefficient conversion of nutrients from plants to animal foods, such as meat and dairy. For example, producing one kilogram of beef requires 25 kilograms of feed crops – with only 3.8 per cent of the protein content and 1.9 per cent of the calories of the feed crops converted to beef (Harwatt *et al.*, 2022). In November 2022, the world's population reached eight billion. Growing food exclusively for people to eat, rather than feeding it to farmed animals, could feed an additional four billion people, that's a total of 12 billion, with less damage to the environment (Cassidy *et al.*, 2013). This is more than the projected two to three billion population growth expected by 2050.

When plant foods are fed to animals, most of the protein and energy they contain are used up in metabolic processes, building bones, cartilage and offal or lost in faeces. As 'food production machines' animals are extremely polluting and inefficient. We all know how wasteful old gas-guzzling cars are – how long before animal agriculture is viewed in the same way?

Over a third of global cereal crops are fed to farmed animals – on a vegan diet an additional four billion people could be fed with 75 per cent less farmland required.

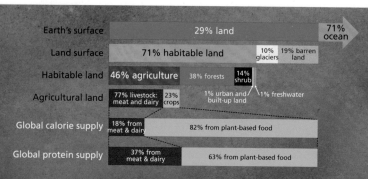

Figure 7. Global land use for food production

Source: Poore and Nemecek, 2018.

Globally, 42 per cent of cereal production is used for feeding farmed animals. In many countries, a much higher proportion is used; 83 per cent in Canada, 81 per cent in the US, 73 per cent in Germany, 68 per cent in France, 61 per cent in Italy and 58 per cent in the UK (Harwatt *et al.*, 2022). This is wasteful, unsustainable and represents a "staggeringly inefficient use of resources" (Bailey *et al.*, 2014).

Poore and Nemecek's 2018 landmark study (discussed above) revealed that meat, fish, dairy and egg production uses around 80 per cent of global farmland and produces 60 per cent of food's greenhouse gas emissions but, as figure 7 shows, provides just 18 per cent of the calories we eat and 37 per cent of the protein (Poore and Nemecek, 2018). In case you are wondering why farmland is used to produce fish – it's because farmed fish (which now surpass wild catch) are fed cereal crops, including soya. So convinced was co-author Joseph Poore by the evidence of how damaging animal agriculture is, that he went vegan himself!

Global meat and dairy consumption is growing faster than cereal consumption. If we don't take fast and drastic action to reduce meat consumption, on current trends, by 2050, more crops could be fed to animals than people (Bailey et al., 2014). If everyone in the world ate the current diet of wealthy industrialised countries, we would need additional land area roughly equivalent to the combined size of Africa and Australia to support livestock production (Eisen and Brown, 2022).

On the other hand, if people stopped eating meat, dairy and other animal products, global farmland could be reduced by more than 75 per cent (Poore and Nemecek, 2018). No grazing land would be needed and less land would be needed to grow crops as humans would be the only ones eating them. Some cropland previously used for animal feed would need to be repurposed to grow crops for people, but there would be an overall massive reduction in land use and we would be able to produce enough food to feed everyone.

In 2019, a study from Harvard Law School researchers found that if all UK cropland was used to grow crops for humans to eat, we could produce more than enough protein and calories for the entire population. This would mean that all UK grazing land could be repurposed, and if restored to native forest, this would offset nine years' worth of current UK emissions (Harwatt and Hayek, 2019).

Similarly, Europe can grow enough plant protein to feed all its people, but not all its farmed animals. Around 80 per cent of the protein fed to animals in Europe is imported from other countries, including developing ones. This plays an important role in the impoverishment of these countries and the exploitation of their environmental resources (Baroni et al., 2007).

Joseph Poore describes how "Converting grass into [meat] is like converting coal to energy. It comes with an immense cost in emissions." Livestock farming will inevitably join the industries like coal, that once boomed but are no longer productive nor desirable. There is much that governments can do to speed up the transition towards a more sustainable diet, they just need to stop ignoring the science!

Water use

Water covers 70 per cent of the world's surface but only three per cent of it is freshwater and much of that is unavailable, trapped in glaciers and snowfields, leaving only one per cent available for humans to use from reservoirs, lakes, rivers and underground sources called aquifers.

Four billion people already struggle to find water for at least one month each year and over two billion live in countries where supply is inadequate. UNICEF say that by 2040, some 600 million children – one in four children worldwide – will be living in areas of extremely high water stress, when demand exceeds availability (UNICEF, 2022).

Water shortages are one of the most dangerous challenges facing the world and it is now commonly said that future wars are more likely to be fought over water than over oil. We simply can't afford to waste water.

Figure 8 shows how agriculture is the single biggest global consumer of freshwater, using 70 per cent of it. Nineteen per cent is used by industry and 11 per cent in the municipal sector – the water we use in households and public services for drinking, cleaning, washing and cooking (FAO, 2021).

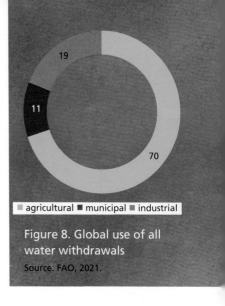

agricultural ■ municipal ■ industrial

Figure 8. Global use of all water withdrawals

Source: FAO, 2021.

Livestock's hidden thirst

Between a third and 40 per cent of the water used in agriculture is used to produce animal products (Gerbens-Leenes *et al.*, 2013; Heinke *et al.*, 2020). Most of that is not drinking water for the animals; around 98 per cent of it is used to grow animal feed crops (Mekonnen and Hoekstra, 2010). Remember, more than a third of the world's crops are used for animal feed and as we've shown, using land to grow feed crops for livestock, rather than food for direct consumption by people, is a waste of resources. The water used on this land represents yet another wasted resource.

Chatham House's research paper *Livestock – Climate Change's Forgotten Sector* says the production of a kilogram of beef, pork and chicken uses around nine, four and three times more water respectively than that of cereals. The report says intensive livestock farming places a strain on scarce surface and groundwater resources and concludes: "A global shift in diets away from livestock products could free significant water resources" (Bailey *et al.*, 2014).

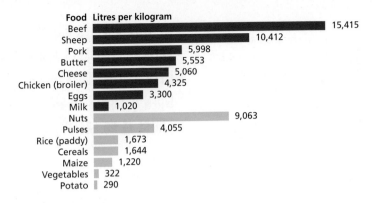

Figure 9. The water footprints of different foods

Source: (Mekonnen and Hoekstra, 2010; Mekonnen and Hoekstra 2012).
To compare the water footprints of more foods, see:
waterfootprint.org/en/resources/interactive-tools/product-gallery

A note on nuts: nuts appear to have a relatively high water footprint but they are packed with protein and healthy unsaturated fat so you only need a small handful to fill you up. Also, they grow on trees, which store carbon and help combat global heating, which is why nuts are listed at the very bottom of Table 1, showing the greenhouse gas emissions for different foods.

The water footprint of different foods

The water footprint of food measures the amount of water used to produce it. The 'water we eat' through the food we consume is much more than what we drink, according to the FAO, who says that depending on your diet, it takes 2,000 to 5,000 litres of water to produce the food consumed daily by one person (FAO, 2022a). As shown in Figure 9, animal-based foods tend to have a considerably higher water footprint than plant-based foods.

Animal agriculture is a major cause of water scarcity. Farming accounts for 70 per cent of all water withdrawals and up to 95 per cent in some developing countries (FAO, 2022a). Your choice of food greatly impacts the amount of water that is needed. Climate change is already altering weather patterns and water availability around the world, causing shortages and droughts in some areas and floods in others. At the current consumption rate, the climate crisis, fuelled by animal agriculture, will worsen water scarcity.

"WE WILL HAVE TO USE OUR NATURAL RESOURCES MORE WISELY AS TIME GOES ON AND WHEN IT COMES TO WATER THERE IS NO EXCEPTION"

(FAO, 2022a).

It will be impossible to feed future generations on the same type of meat and dairy-rich diets typical in Western Europe and North America. Rich countries have been able to buy their way out of the problem to some degree by importing 'virtual water', that is either meat or livestock feed crops from other countries, even from water-poor ones. Many countries have moved their water footprint oversees in this way without considering whether the imported products are contributing to water depletion or pollution in the producing countries. Therefore, a vegan diet would play an important role in preserving water and reducing hunger and malnutrition in poorer nations (Baroni et al., 2007).

Reducing animal-based foods in the diet offers the potential to save enough water to feed 1.8 billion additional people globally (Jalava et al., 2014). Is that meaty burger more important than the large number of people, typically women and girls, who have to walk for hours every day just to fetch water? There are so many great plant-based alternatives available now – there really is no need to waste precious water growing crops to feed farmed animals.

Deforestation

Ten thousand years ago, forests covered more than half of the Earth's habitable land, they now account for less than a third (31 per cent) and that amount is shrinking (FAO, 2022b). Between 1990 and 2020, 420 million hectares of forest were lost due to deforestation, an area the size of the EU (FAO, 2020). The FAO says that despite deforestation rates falling, 10 million hectares of forest were lost each year between 2015 and 2020 (FAO, 2022b). One hectare is about the size of a European football field or Trafalgar Square in London.

NOT ON TRACK TO MEET CLIMATE TARGETS

The Forest Declaration Assessment publishes annual progress reports on the state of global forests. In their 2022 report, they say global deforestation slowed by six per cent compared to the average rate between 2018 and 2020 (Forest Declaration Assessment Partners, 2022). This falls short of the annual 10 per cent cut needed to end deforestation by 2030 – the target agreed by over 100 world leaders at COP26 in Glasgow.

Agricultural expansion – the biggest driver

The United Nations says that agricultural expansion is the single biggest driver of deforestation, driving almost 90 per cent of global forest losses. It says 52 per cent of these losses are from expansion for cropland (including animal feed crops) and 38 per cent is from expansion for livestock grazing (FAO, 2022b). However, in many parts of the world, such as South America and Oceania, livestock grazing is the biggest driver of deforestation (FAO, 2022b).

When land is cleared, there are fewer trees to take carbon from the atmosphere and if trees are burned or left to rot, more carbon is released. This disastrous double-whammy is why deforestation accounts for around 11 per cent of all global greenhouse gas emissions (IPCC, 2014). In the Amazon, fire-driven deforestation is the main source of carbon emissions (van Marle et al., 2017).

A THIRD OF THE PLANET'S LAND AREA HAS BEEN TRANSFORMED IN THE LAST 60 YEARS, AND NEARLY 90 PER CENT OF DEFORESTATION BETWEEN 2000 AND 2018 WAS RELATED TO AGRICULTURE (FAO, 2022b).

In Europe, North America and Northeast Asia, some gains in forest land have been made along with reductions in agricultural land. However, in many of these regions, imports of animal foods have increased – so the problem has simply been moved elsewhere. This does nothing to reduce global emissions nor combat climate change. Globally, deforestation may have slowed in the last decade, but it remains alarmingly high in many parts of the world.

Brazil is home to around 60 per cent of the Amazon rainforest, the world's largest rainforest. Its preservation is vital to protect planet Earth against catastrophic climate change because of the vast amounts of greenhouse gases it absorbs. More than 20 per cent of Amazon forest has been replaced by pasture and cropland since the early 1970s. After decades of severe deforestation, the rate of forest loss slowed but, since 2012, the rate has picked up again due to a relaxed policy and accelerated agricultural development (Jiang *et al.*, 2020).

In Brazil, clearing land for beef production is the big driver, says Dr Erika Berenguer, from the University of Oxford, rather than for timber or making space to produce palm oil or soya (most of which is used for animal feed). "Typically," Berenguer says, "gangs use a chain slung between two tractors to knock down trees quickly and at an industrial scale. Once the felled trees are dry enough, they are burned to leave the ground clear for cattle ranching" (Vaughan, 2019).

Between August 2020 and July 2021, deforestation in Brazil's Amazon rainforest rose by almost 22 per cent, the highest level in 15 years, according to Brazil's space research agency, INPE. They say an area of land 13,235 square kilometres (5,110 square miles) was lost – that's an area nearly 17 times the size of New York City (Spring and Boadle, 2021). Scientists fear that the world's biggest rainforest is approaching a tipping point beyond which it may not be able to recover.

Illegal deforestation and land grabbing

In the report *Illicit Harvest, Complicit Goods*, it's revealed how many agricultural products exported worldwide from Latin America, Southeast Asia and Africa are linked back to illegal deforestation (Dummett and Blundell, 2021). It found that between 2013 and 2019, 69 per cent of tropical deforestation for commercial agriculture was done illegally. During this time, illegal 'agro-conversion' was responsible for the loss of forest from an area roughly the size of Norway. Because over 30 per cent of agricultural goods linked to deforestation are exported, there must be significant concerns about the links to illegal deforestation (Dummett and Blundell, 2021).

The report also found that emissions from illegal agro-conversion account for over 40 per cent of emissions from tropical deforestation (Dummett and Blundell, 2021). "We should all be shocked that illegal clearing for commercial agriculture is the largest driver of deforestation – and that it's getting bigger. If we don't urgently stop this unlawful deforestation, we don't have a chance to beat the three crises facing humanity: climate change, biodiversity loss and emerging pandemics" said lead co-author Art Blundell.

When forests are cleared for crops, much of them are grown for animal feed. Most of the soya grown in Latin America, for example, is used for animal feed to fuel the global supply of animal-based fast foods. The non-profit organisation TABLE (successor to the Food Climate Research Network), says that the vast majority of the UK's soya imports come from South America and only a paltry 20 to 30 per cent are certified as deforestation free.

TABLE estimates that at least 90 per cent of imported soya in the UK is fed to animals. A lot of this is used in poultry and pork production, but beef, dairy and aquaculture are also responsible for a considerable amount of UK soya consumption (TABLE, 2022). There is little traceability, so the direct link between a chicken tikka masala or a bacon butty eaten in London, for example, and deforestation of the Amazon are lost to many.

In 2021, an investigation by the Bureau of Investigative Journalism found that beef from farmers accused of illegal deforestation in Brazil

was finding its way into major global suppliers whose UK customers include Sainsbury's, Asda, Lidl and other major supermarkets and wholesalers

BRITISH HUNGER FOR MEAT DRIVING DEFORESTATION IN BRAZIL

(Bureau of Investigative Journalism, 2021). Previously, an investigation by the same group found that Britain's leading supermarkets and fast food outlets, including Tesco, Asda, Lidl, Nando's and McDonald's, were all selling chicken fed on soya linked to vast deforestation of the Amazon (Bureau of Investigative Journalism, 2021a). The only way to be sure you are not supporting deforestation is to avoid all animal-based foods and go vegan!

Changing what we eat could have a phenomenal impact on reducing deforestation and combating climate change. Researchers from the Institute of Social Ecology in Vienna say that if the world went vegan, it would be possible to produce enough food for everyone in 2050 without another single tree being cut down (Erb *et al.*, 2016). That means zero deforestation. If the land used previously for grazing animals was allowed to revert to forest, the carbon captured and held by trees could be large enough to cancel out up to 300 years of food-related greenhouse gas emissions (Bryngelsson *et al.*, 2016).

Why forests matter

Often referred to as the 'lungs' of the Earth, trees store carbon and release oxygen. They store 80 per cent of the total aboveground carbon in land-based ecosystems in their trunks, branches and leaves and 40 per cent of the belowground carbon in their roots (Li *et al*. 2018). Trees also stabilise soil and reduce flooding. By pulling water from the ground and emitting it from their leaves, tropical forests provide local cooling. One study estimates that tropical forests may cool Earth by a whole 1°C (Lawrence *et al*., 2022). Preserving forests is crucial for combatting global heating. Without trees, it's unlikely that we would survive.

Deforestation and zoonoses

Forests are diverse and dynamic places, hosting a quarter of the world's biodiversity. They provide a habitat for 80 per cent of amphibian species, 75 per cent of bird species and 68 per cent of mammal species (FAO, 2022b).

More than 28,000 different plant species are used in medicines and many of them come from forests. We risk losing valuable future medicines if deforestation continues. Yet, forests also pose health risks as encroaching into forest wildlife habitats increases human exposure to new and existing infectious diseases. Most new infectious diseases, including covid and mpox (previously known as monkeypox), are zoonotic – they come from animals. Forest-associated zoonotic diseases include malaria, Chagas disease, African trypanosomiasis (sleeping sickness), leishmaniasis, Lyme disease, HIV and Ebola (FAO and UNEP, 2020). There will be more.

Scientists agree that if we are seriously going to attempt to limit global heating to 1.5°C above pre-industrial levels – the threshold beyond which Earth's climate will become profoundly disrupted – deforestation must end. Not only would this combat climate change, but it would also generate multiple other local and global benefits – such as biodiversity conservation, the protection of soils and water and maintaining pollination services (FAO, 2022b). In other words, the entire future of humanity depends on it!

There is no question that the global demand for animal-based foods will continue to rise unless we actively promote changing our diet to move away from these products. There is a clear need for a strategic, integrated approach to agriculture, forestry and other policies linked to how we use the planet's limited natural resources.

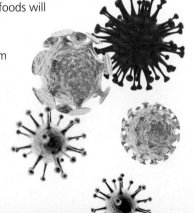

Pollution

It's hard to imagine the monumental quantities of fertilisers and pesticides used on the millions of acres of cropland needed to feed the 80 billion land animals killed every year for food. Now try to imagine the amount of manure they produce – it is seven to nine times more sewage than humans produce, and most of it is left untreated! Just in the UK, dairy cows produce 50 billion litres of manure a year and over 300 incidents of river pollution were reported in 2021, with only six prosecutions. Because of this, animal agriculture is a major contributor to land, water and air pollution, prompting some scientists to say we need to stop eating meat and dairy.

Water pollution

"The livestock sector is growing and intensifying faster than crop production in almost all countries. The associated waste, including manure, has serious implications for water quality" (FAO, 2017).

The fact that animal agriculture uses 75 per cent of all agricultural land gives some indication of the huge amount of pollution that arises from it. Around 80 billion land animals are killed for meat every year alongside many trillions of fish and shellfish (FAOSTAT, 2022).

An investigation of agrochemical industry data found that crops grown mainly for animal feed are a driving force in the global market for hazardous pesticides (Unearthed, 2020). More than $23bn of pesticide sales data from 2018 was analysed and almost half of it was listed on the Pesticide Action Network International 2019 list of highly hazardous pesticides. Close to half of those were sprayed on just two crops: soya beans and maize. An estimated three-quarters of the world's soya and maize production ends up as animal feed for the meat industry, particularly for chickens and pigs. Furthermore, most of the soya grown for animal feed had been genetically modified to be resistant to herbicides like glyphosate, allowing these chemicals to be used more intensively.

Aquaculture – factory farming fish – has grown more than 20-fold since the 1980s, particularly in Asia (FAO and IWMI, 2017). Fish excreta and uneaten fish feed from aquaculture diminish water quality. Increased production has combined with greater use of antibiotics, fungicides and anti-fouling agents, which also contribute to polluting downstream ecosystems.

UNDER PRESSURE FROM AGRICULTURAL POLLUTION

Excessive amounts of fertiliser and manure from animal agriculture are contributing to a major environmental problem called 'eutrophication'. The term comes from the Greek eutrophos, meaning well-nourished. But this is not a good thing; polluting water with excess nutrients from fertilisers and manure promotes the growth of harmful algae that lead to aquatic dead zones. Globally, 415 coastal areas have been identified as experiencing some form of

Four steps of eutrophication

1. **EXCESS NUTRIENTS:** from fertiliser or manure entering the water
2. **ALGAE BLOOM:** nitrogen and phosphorus from the fertiliser/manure promote the growth of algae in water
3. **OXYGEN DEPLETION:** algal blooms block sunlight from entering water, preventing photosynthesis in water plants and the water becomes oxygen-depleted. Algae also release toxins that poison wildlife and lead to a loss of biodiversity
4. **DEAD ZONES:** water is completely depleted of oxygen, fish suffocate and it becomes a dead zone, no longer able to support life

eutrophication, of which 169 are hypoxic – having too little oxygen (FAO and IWMI, 2017).

Fertilisers and manure (either overflowing from lagoons, excessively spread on land or directly dumped into waterways) are the leading cause of high levels of nutrients in some aquatic environments. These harmful practices have led to the pollution of inland water bodies and coastal waters. The FAO says: "Nitrate from agriculture is now the most common chemical contaminant in the world's groundwater aquifers" (FAO and IWMI, 2017).

"The increase in demand for food with high environmental footprints, such as meat from industrial farms, is contributing to unsustainable agricultural intensification and to water-quality degradation" (FAO and IWMI, 2017).

"In the European Union, 38 per cent of water bodies are significantly under pressure from agricultural pollution" says the FAO, and in the US, "agriculture is the main source of pollution in rivers and streams" (FAO and IWMI, 2017). In China, the direct discharge of animal manure into waterbodies remains widely practised and is a significant

cause of pollution with more than half the freshwater lakes now polluted (Strokal *et al.*, 2016).

There has been a dramatic global rise in fish farming (aquaculture) in marine, brackish-water (saltier than freshwater but not as much as seawater) and freshwater environments (FAO and IWMI, 2017). This increased production has combined with the greater use of antibiotics, fungicides and anti-fouling agents, which along with fish waste (excreta) and uneaten fish feed, are polluting downstream ecosystems, further reducing water quality (FAO and IWMI, 2017).

In the last 20 years, a new class of agricultural pollutants has emerged with veterinary medicines, such as antibiotics and hormonal growth promoters, moving from farms to water. Zoonotic waterborne pathogens are yet another major concern (FAO and IWMI, 2017). Until the demand for animal products decreases, water pollution will continue. We can protect our waterways by shifting to a vegan diet.

Air pollution

Air pollution causes over six million deaths a year globally and this number is increasing (Fuller *et al.*, 2022). Most people think industry and transport are the main cause, but animal agriculture is now the major driver in many parts of the world.

The problem is those nitrogen-containing fertilisers and manure again. They can emit significant quantities of nitrogen-containing gases, including ammonia for example, that combine with pollution from industry or transport to form particulate matter (PM) so tiny it can invade even the smallest airways in the lungs of children and adults. Evidence suggests that this is a leading cause of air pollution in Europe, much of the US, Russia and China (Bauer *et al.*, 2016).

PM2.5 has a diameter smaller than 2.5 micrometres – the average human hair is about 70 micrometres wide – making it 30 times larger. The potential of PM2.5 for harming health is linked to its size; it can stick in the fine lung tissue causing breathing difficulties, damage heart and lung function and can cause premature death. Scientists say "more emphasis on reducing emissions in Europe would have marked benefits in reducing episodic PM2.5 concentrations in the UK" (Vieno *et al.*, 2016).

Air pollution from animal agriculture can be very localised too. Asthma, bronchitis, chronic obstructive airways disease and other lung diseases may affect as many as

LUNG DISEASES MAY AFFECT UP TO A THIRD OF FACTORY FARM WORKERS

30 per cent of factory farm workers (Hribar and Schultz, 2010). Research shows that even people who live near industrial farms have a much greater risk of asthma and other disease of the airways and lungs (Schultz *et al.*, 2019).

As the world's appetite for meat, fish, eggs and dairy continues to grow, emissions from livestock continue to rise. Reducing meat, fish, dairy and egg production means reducing air pollution – and that could mean the difference between life and death for millions of people every year.

Wildlife loss

While a lot of attention is rightly given to the climate crisis, there is another crisis unfolding: wildlife loss. We are now living through the world's sixth mass extinction and the United Nations says that one million species are at risk of becoming extinct (IPBES, 2019). Conservation ecologist, Stuart Pimm, of Duke University in Durham, North Carolina, says that we are losing species at 1,000 times the natural rate (Pimm *et al.*, 2014). Unlike previous extinction events that were caused by asteroids, volcanic eruptions and natural climate shifts, this crisis is caused by human activity with animal agriculture at the heart of it.

The International Union for Conservation of Nature's (IUCN) Red List of Threatened Species is a useful indicator of the health of the world's biodiversity – a barometer of life. To date, more than 147,500 species have been assessed by the IUCN and more than 41,000 (28 per cent) of them are threatened with extinction, many within decades (IUCN, 2022). Figure 10 shows the percentages of certain species under threat, including 27 per cent of mammals and 13 per cent of birds.

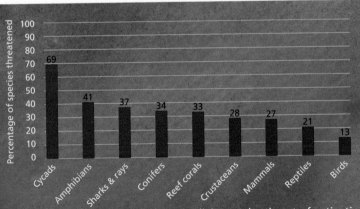

Figure 10. The percentage of species living under threat of extinction

Source: IUCN, 2022. (Cycads are ancient palm-like plants).

The conversion of forests and grasslands to intensive agriculture and livestock farming is the single biggest direct driver of wildlife loss globally. Other factors such as hunting, pollution and climate change also have impacts, but the principal driver is animal agriculture (Jaureguiberry *et al.*, 2022).

ANIMAL AGRICULTURE IS THE SINGLE LARGEST DRIVER OF WILDLIFE LOSS

Overexploitation, agriculture and aquaculture are the main threats to wildlife – the expansion of agriculture alone threatens 62 per cent of endangered species (Maxwell *et al.*, 2016).

When natural ecosystems are cleared to make way for agriculture, the wildlife that live there lose their homes or are killed. Over the last 50 years, the conversion of ecosystems for crop production or pasture has been the principal cause of habitat destruction and biodiversity loss (Benton *et al.*, 2021).

"The consumption of animal-sourced food products by humans is one of the most powerful negative forces affecting the conservation of terrestrial ecosystems and biological diversity" (Machovina *et al.*, 2015).

What is biodiversity and how many species are there on Earth?

Biodiversity refers to the amazing variety of all life on Earth – from tiny microorganisms to gigantic animals and towering trees. We don't know how many different species inhabit the planet, but it's estimated to be around nine million and only 14 per cent on land and nine per cent in the oceans have been classified (Mora *et al.*, 2011). We face losing many species before they have even been identified.

42

A rich biodiversity is vital for our survival; complex ecosystems produce oxygen, filter water, recycle nutrients,

generate soil and pollinate seeds. Birds, bats, butterflies, bees and other pollinators support over three-quarters of global food crops, including coffee, cocoa and almonds (FAO, 2018). The air we breathe, water we drink, food we eat and medicines we depend on, all rely heavily on biodiversity. David Macdonald, professor of wildlife conservation at the University of Oxford says: "Without biodiversity, there is no future for humanity."

A world out of balance

The imbalance of life on Earth is staggering. By weight, 60 per cent of mammals on the planet are livestock, 36 per cent are humans and just four per cent are wild creatures (Bar-On et al., 2018). There are over 24 billion chickens in the world – more than three birds for every person. Since 1970, the number of people and livestock has risen massively, but the combined global weight of wild mammals has fallen by a shocking 82 per cent (Benton et al., 2021).

Whichever way you look at it, farmed animals are massively over-represented among the world's living creatures and animal agriculture is destroying the natural world. Such massive livestock populations have profound consequences for biodiversity, including their contribution to climate change, deforestation, change of land use, overgrazing, degradation of grasslands and desertification. Vast areas of cropland are used to produce animal feed, such as soya, maize and palm oil, so meat-eaters globally are directly contributing to this destruction.

As discussed, animal agriculture is also a main driver of the climate crisis (IPBES, 2019). Climate change – leading to storms, flooding, extreme temperatures, drought and sea-level rise – affects nearly one in five threatened or near-threatened species (Maxwell et al., 2016). Land once fertile is becoming arid and unable to support life. Ecosystems that have evolved over thousands of years are breaking down. As animal agriculture and aquaculture expands, the natural world is shrinking.

In marine ecosystems, fishing is the largest driver of biodiversity loss, whereas freshwater wildlife is affected by poor water quality resulting from farm chemical run-off. Pollution from fertilisers and fish farming also damages marine ecosystems. "All in all, our food system is the major factor underpinning reductions in the population sizes of wild species of animals and plants, and the erosion of biodiversity, from the local level to the global level" (Benton et al., 2021).

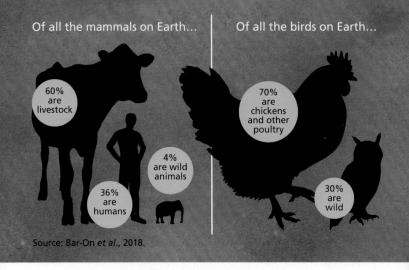

Of all the mammals on Earth…

60% are livestock

36% are humans

4% are wild animals

Of all the birds on Earth…

70% are chickens and other poultry

30% are wild

Source: Bar-On *et al.*, 2018.

Living under threat

Magnificent mammals such as Africa's cheetahs, the UK's hedgehogs and water voles and the hooded seals of the cold waters of the North Atlantic and Arctic Oceans are just a handful of those affected, from one side of the planet to the other, by animal agriculture and aquaculture (Maxwell *et al.*, 2016).

Over 40 per cent of the world's insects are in decline having lost their natural habitat to intensive agriculture (Sánchez-Bayo and Wyckhuys, 2019). Anyone who grew up in the 1970s will remember the splattering of dead insects on car windscreens that happened on long journeys. Nowadays, there are hardly any. Experts say intensive agriculture and the increased use of pesticides over the last 50 years are responsible for the massive declines. It's an insect apocalypse! Insects create the biological foundation for a vast array of ecosystems and without them, the entire web of life would become so disrupted that all life on Earth could be placed in jeopardy.

Small animals that live below ground are under threat too; over a third of fields in England are seriously deficient in earthworms and in some fields, they are missing altogether (Stroud, 2019). Birds are sensitive to environmental change and their population numbers can reflect changes in ecosystems and other animal and plant populations. Long-term monitoring in Europe reveals significant population declines, particularly in farmland birds (European Environment Agency, 2021).

Primates are our closest biological relatives and play an essential role in tropical biodiversity, contributing to forest regeneration and ecosystem health. Ring-tailed lemurs in Madagascar, for example, are important seed dispersers but numbers have declined by 45 per cent over the past 40 years (Brinkmann *et al.*, 2014).

Around 60 per cent of primates are threatened with extinction because of habitat loss, agricultural expansion, deforestation, cattle-ranching, hunting for bushmeat and illegal trade as pets or 'medicinal' body parts, and climate change. The expanding production of soya, palm oil and beef is seriously impacting biodiversity and primate populations because these large-scale, commercial monocultures require complete clearing of natural habitats (Estrada *et al.*, 2019). Palm kernel meal is a lucrative by-product of palm oil production and, along with soya, it is used as animal feed with more than a tenth of global production fed to British livestock and companion animals with little, if any, coming from sustainable sources (Defra, 2011).

In both Africa and Asia, populations of great apes – gorillas, chimpanzees, bonobos and orangutans – are rapidly declining. As a result of poaching, loss of habitat to agriculture and infectious diseases, great ape numbers have collapsed. There are less than 1,200 mountain gorillas remaining in the mountainous area straddling the Democratic Republic of Congo, Rwanda and Uganda – the last refuge of mountain gorillas in the world (UNEP, 2021) and the Western chimpanzee, found in West Africa, is now also critically endangered (IUCN, 2022). In Asia, all three species of orangutans are listed as critically endangered (IUCN, 2022).

Decades of habitat loss, poaching and conflict have also devastated African elephant populations, with only around 350,000 remaining compared to the 10 million that roamed the continent as recently as 1930 (Chase *et al.*, 2016).

Trees are a valuable carbon sink and store around 40 per cent of all land carbon while producing up to 20 per cent of the world's oxygen – mostly from rainforests. In terms of biodiversity, the Amazon rainforest is the richest region on Earth and is one of the last refuges for many animals, including jaguars and pink river dolphins. It is home to sloths, black spider monkeys and poison dart frogs and perhaps a million more undiscovered species. According to the United Nations, animal agriculture is the principal global driver of deforestation because of the extent to which forests are being converted to farmland for grazing and animal feed crops (UN News, 2019).

Almost a decade ago, Gidon Eshel, then professor of environmental physics at Bard College, said: "You eat a steak, you kill a lemur in Madagascar. You eat a chicken, you kill an Amazonian parrot" (Morell, 2015). Each bite fuels mass species extinction and drives global deforestation. When choosing a meat burger, you are eating the Earth. Choose vegan instead.

Grasslands and savannahs are also being destroyed for meat production and a typical example is the African savannah, home to a huge variety of mammals, reptiles, amphibians and birds. Roaming elephants and buffalo, grasshoppers and beetles, ants and termites make up an extraordinarily complex and diverse ecosystem that has evolved over thousands of years, but which is now under threat, with many native animals becoming endangered.

In the oceans, over a third of wild fish are now overfished, compared to 10 per cent in 1974 (FAO, 2020a). Larger fish are being squeezed from both ends; under threat from overfishing and under pressure as numbers at the bottom of the food chain decrease due to climate change. Without significant changes, more than half of the world's marine species may face extinction by the end of this century (UNESCO, 2017).

Coral reefs support more than a quarter of all marine life but around half of all shallow water corals have already been lost due to overfishing and rising sea temperatures and up to 90 per cent could be gone by 2050 (WWF, 2018). As atmospheric carbon dioxide

dissolves in the ocean, it increases acidity and organisms whose shells are made from calcium carbonate have to work hard at strengthening their shells just to survive!

Seagrasses play a vital role in coastal ecosystems, but they too are under threat from destructive fishing practices, climate change and contamination from farmland run-off. They have been disappearing at a rate of 110 square kilometres a year since 1980 and have disappeared from almost a third of the area they inhabited in the late 1800s. These losses are comparable to those seen in coral reefs and tropical rainforests and place seagrass meadows among the most threatened ecosystems on Earth (Waycott *et al.*, 2009).

Marine microalgae (phytoplankton) not only store carbon when they die and sink to the ocean floor but also provide half of all the Earth's oxygen. Their numbers are falling by one per cent a year (Boyce *et al.*, 2010; Gregg *et al.*, 2017) adding yet another layer – along with coral bleaching due to oceanic warming caused by the climate crisis, overfishing and acidification – to the relentless barrage of assaults the world's oceans are facing.

Biodiversity loss in the UK

The UK is one of the most nature-depleted countries in the world with around one in six native species threatened with extinction (Hayhow *et al.*, 2019). A quarter of mammals and nearly half of all birds in the UK are at risk – hedgehogs, hares, bats and birds, such as the willow tit and turtle dove, and insects, such as the high brown fritillary butterfly are all living under threat.

A QUARTER OF UK MAMMALS AND NEARLY HALF OF ALL BIRDS ARE AT RISK

The 'usual culprits' are responsible – intensification of farming, use of pesticides and fertilisers, higher stocking densities for sheep and cattle, greater mechanisation and the loss of field margins, hedgerows, wooded areas and farm ponds. The clear trend is of increasing agricultural productivity linked to negative consequences for wildlife (Hayhow *et al.*, 2019).

In the UK, bees, butterflies, dragonflies, grasshoppers, beetles, hoverflies, spiders and wasps are moving north at an average rate of two kilometres a year due to increased temperatures from climate change (Platts *et al.*, 2019). This is happening in other countries too – over half of plant and animal species in temperate North America are moving away from hotter into cooler places (Weiskopf *et al.*, 2020).

In 2020, the Red List for British Mammals revealed that 11 of the 47 mammals native to Britain are on the brink of extinction, while a further five species are classified as near threatened (Mammal Society, 2020). Among those listed as being at risk are the water vole, hedgehog, hazel dormouse, wildcat and the grey long-eared bat. The European wolf is already extinct.

Ancient woodlands are the richest and most complex habitat in the UK – home to more threatened species than any other, including unique and complex communities of delicate fungi, rare mosses and special flowering plants that only thrive in that environment. Specialist 'ecological indicator' species such as lichens, bluebells, wild garlic and hart's-tongue ferns show that a site has been wooded for a long time (Woodland Trust, 2020).

Once dominating the British landscape, ancient woodlands have been reduced to covering just a tiny fraction (2.4 per cent) of Britain's land area.

ANCIENT WOODLANDS NOW COVER A TINY FRACTION OF BRITAIN

While there has been a small increase in woodland cover over the past few decades, the trend for ancient woods, and wildlife found there, is in steep decline (Reid *et al.*, 2021).

While building and infrastructure projects are largely to blame, an increasing threat comes from ammonia released from intensive pig and poultry farms (Woodland Trust, 2020). Ammonia (NH_3) is a form of nitrogen air pollution affecting woods. Agriculture accounts for 88 per cent of UK ammonia emissions, with most coming from livestock manure. This type of nitrogen air pollution strips trees of their protective lichens and causes a fertiliser effect allowing grasses to out-compete more delicate woodland flowers (Reid *et al.*, 2021).

We need to protect ancient woodlands and reduce their exposure to pollution. However, there are an increasing number of US-style mega-farms appearing in the UK. These largescale intensive facilities house at least 2,500 pigs or 120,000 chickens and generate vast quantities of animal waste. There are now more than 1,000 mega-farms in England, Wales and Northern Ireland, including some holding as many as a million animals (Lymbery, 2022).

UK MEGA—FARMS HOLDING AS MANY AS A MILLION ANIMALS

The idea that sheep grazing on the hillsides is a 'natural' scene couldn't be further from the truth. Two centuries of sheep farming, particularly on upland soils, has reduced a rich natural resource to a state of desolation. A 2020 study from the University of Liverpool showed how sheep grazing negatively affects the diversity of plant species of upland areas in Britain. They suggest that even if grazing stops, some areas could take up to 60 years to recover (Marrs *et al.*, 2020).

But we can't eat grass, so we might as well let sheep graze and then we can eat them – or so the argument goes. If UK cropland, for example, was used to grow plants for people rather than feeding animals, we could feed everyone in the UK and most grazing land could be restored to native forest, which would offset nine years' worth of UK emissions (Harwatt and Hayek, 2019). Even if land isn't suitable for arable crops – natural scrub land or peat bogs, for example, are more beneficial to the environment than grazed grassland.

Whichever way you look at it, the most effective way to protect UK wildlife is to stop eating animals and go vegan.

Scientists recommend that people reduce their consumption of animal foods, replacing them with more sustainable plant foods, and say a future with a lower demand for meat, fish, eggs and dairy would drastically reduce habitat and biodiversity loss, fossil fuel energy use, greenhouse gas emissions and pollution while providing a nutritious diet that could greatly improve global health (Machovina *et al.*, 2015).

We must make the connection between animal agriculture and environmental destruction, protect ecosystems and prioritise the safety and freedom of wild animals. If we don't take urgent and far-reaching action now, eating animals will be the death of us.

To find out more about how animal agriculture is killing wildlife go to viva.org.uk/eating-the-earth

Overfishing and fish farming

Over the last 50 years, the world's population has doubled and so has the appetite for fish, effectively increasing the amount of fish eaten fourfold. In 1961, the average person ate nine kilograms of fish a year, that increased to over 20 kilograms in 2018 (FAO, 2020a).

Overfishing is when more fish are caught than the population can replace through natural reproduction. It impacts individual species, communities and entire ocean ecosystems. The FAO says the percentage of stocks fished at unsustainable levels increased from 10 per cent in 1974 to 35 per cent in 2019 (FAO, 2022c). This is putting pressure on fisheries around the world. A fishery is an area where fish and shellfish are caught for commercial purposes. The number of fisheries collapsing is increasing and if trends continue, 88 per cent will be overfished by 2050 (Costello *et al.*, 2016).

DRASTIC DECLINES HAVE BEEN SEEN ACROSS ENTIRE COMMUNITIES

"From giant blue marlin to mighty bluefin tuna, and from tropical groupers to Antarctic cod, industrial fishing has scoured the global ocean. There is no blue frontier left" says Ransom Myers, a world-leading fisheries biologist based at Dalhousie University in Canada

Percentage of fish stocks fished at unsustainable levels

10 per cent in 1974

35 per cent in 2019

88 per cent by 2050

(FAO, 2022c; Costello *et al.*, 2016).

(SeaWeb, 2003). Myers' research found that 90 per cent of all large fish, including tuna, marlin, swordfish, sharks, groupers, cod and halibut, are gone. His study found that industrial fisheries take only 10 to 15 years to grind any new fish community they encounter down to a tenth of what it was before. These drastic declines have been seen across entire communities in widely varying ecosystems (Myers and Worm, 2003).

"Industrial fisheries are now going thousands of miles, thousands of feet deep and catching things that live hundreds of years in the process – in the least protected place on Earth" says Elliott Norse of the Marine Conservation Biology Institute (SeaWeb, 2007). Many of these fish living in the depths of the ocean take 30 or 40 years to reach maturity and breed, so when too many of them are caught, there is no way to replenish their population. In many cases, fish caught today are under such intense pressure, they don't even get the chance to reproduce. It's like chopping down ancient oak trees, except that we cannot 'replant' them!

Disrupting ocean ecosystems

When too many fish and other animals are taken out of the ocean it creates an imbalance, the consequences of which can be far-reaching. Commercial whaling, which started over 50 years ago in the North Pacific, provides an example of how disrupting ecosystems can set off complex chain reactions with unexpected results (Springer *et al.*, 2003).

KILLING THE LARGEST ANIMALS IN THE OCEANS MAY DISRUPT ECOSYSTEMS FOR MILLIONS OF YEARS

Tens of millions of whales have been killed and populations have fallen by 66 to 90 per cent (Roman *et al.*, 2014). As a result of this mass slaughter, orcas that predated whales turned to smaller marine mammals like seals and sea otters. The decline of sea otters, in turn, enabled their prey, sea urchins, to increase and feast on kelp forests. Just as forests on land support biodiversity and combat climate change by absorbing and storing carbon, kelp forests in the ocean serve the same function (Filbee-Dexter, 2020). A reduction in kelp forests means an increase in atmospheric carbon dioxide – driving global heating. Scientists say removing the largest animals from the oceans is unprecedented in the history of animal life and may disrupt ecosystems for millions of years (Payne *et al.*, 2016).

DON'T EAT FISH AS OLD AS YOUR GRANDMA!

Previously known as slimeheads, the orange roughy was largely ignored by the commercial fishing industry until the decline in cod and haddock and the advances in trawling technology made it viable to target this deep-sea fish. This led to a 'gold rush' mentality – wherever orange roughy was found it was fished intensively. These fish don't reproduce until they are 20 to 30 years old and can live to be 150 or more. "When you buy orange roughy at the store, you are probably purchasing a filet from a fish that is at least 50 years old" says Selena Heppell, Head of the Department of Fisheries Wildlife and Conservation Sciences at Oregon State University. "Most people don't think of the implications of that. Perhaps we need a guideline that says we shouldn't eat fish that are as old as our grandmothers" (Goudarzi, 2007).

Bottom trawling

Bottom trawling is the world's most destructive type of fishing that herds and captures target species, such as ground fish, by dragging gigantic nets across the ocean floor. It is one of the most common methods of fishing in the world and accounts for half of the UK's annual fish catch.

NETS BIG ENOUGH TO SWALLOW A BOEING 747 JUMBO JET!

Trawl nets can be 450 feet long. The mouths of the largest nets are big enough to swallow a Boeing 747 jumbo jet! This fishing method is indiscriminate, sweeping up all species in its path. Imagine the damage a net this large does as it drags across the seabed catching everything in its path. European scientists have calculated that bottom trawlers in the North Sea destroy 16 pounds of marine animals for every pound of marketable sole that is caught (Danson and D'Orso, 2011). "Undoubtedly, the greatest and most irreversible damage is due to the increasing intensity of deep-water trawling that relies on the deployment of heavy gear which 'steamrollers' over the sea floor" (UNEP, 2004).

"Demersal [bottom of the sea] fishing gear has destroyed many ancient deep-sea coral reefs in the past 30 years, and none have been restored" (Hilmi *et al*. 2021). Murray Roberts of the Scottish Association for Marine Science says: "In some places skippers have replaced their nets with chains, to take out the corals so they don't tear the nets. Then they go back and scoop up the fish" (SeaWeb, 2007).

Some living corals date back 1,800 years and reefs may be older than the Egyptian pyramids. Roberts says: "If we lose them, we are erasing invaluable historical records and we are not only losing our past – on one coral mound off Ireland we found eight species new to science in just a few samples. These are real biodiversity hotspots" (MCBI, 2007).

FISHING BOATS THAT TRAWL THE OCEAN FLOOR RELEASE AS MUCH CARBON DIOXIDE AS THE ENTIRE AVIATION INDUSTRY

Bottom trawling fishing gear also churns up seabed sediments releasing the 'blue' carbon stored there. Fishing boats that trawl the ocean floor collectively release 0.6 to 1.5 gigatons of carbon dioxide a year, a similar amount as the entire aviation industry's annual emissions, according to a ground-breaking study written by 26 marine biologists, climate experts and economists and published in the journal *Nature* (Sala *et al*., 2021).

Longline fishing

Longline fishing is another popular commercial fishing method that uses long lines with baited hooks attached at intervals. Hundreds or even thousands of hooks can hang from a single line which may be an incredible 28 miles long (NOAA Fisheries, 2019). Longliners commonly target swordfish, tuna, halibut, sablefish and many other species. Japanese longlining has expanded globally and has been likened to a hole burning through paper. As the hole expands, the edge is where the fisheries concentrate until there is nowhere left to go.

Bycatch

Wherever there is fishing, there is bycatch – the unwanted fish and other marine creatures, such as dolphins, sea turtles and seabirds, trapped by commercial fishing nets. They are usually discarded overboard as waste, often dead or dying. In EU waters alone, figures from WWF show that in 2019, 230,000 tonnes of fish were dumped (WWF, 2022). Most of this (92 per cent) was related to bottom-trawling. The capture and disposal of bycatch poses a serious threat to species diversity and ecosystems because this part of a catch is usually unregulated and may make up 30 to 40 per cent of global marine catches (Davies *et al.*, 2009; FAO, 2022c).

Loggerheads and leatherbacks are the species of sea turtle most captured as bycatch in longline fishing. However, high numbers of other sea turtles are also caught worldwide. The hook can penetrate a turtle's flippers, head, mouth or neck. If a turtle swallows the whole hook, it can become lodged in their digestive tract, resulting in starvation and death. Turtles and other sea creatures like this often bleed to death while hanging from longline hooks. If they manage to survive, it's likely they will die when pulled up onto the ship (NOAA Fisheries, 2019).

ILLEGAL FiSHiNG MAY ACCOUNT FOR ONE iN EVERY FiVE FiSH CAUGHT

This is a despicable waste of life that causes the needless loss of billions of fish and hundreds of thousands of sea creatures and seabirds. So, when buying fish, shellfish or even fish fingers – the purchase is not only responsible for the death of that fish but, sadly, for the deaths of many other sea creatures too.

Illegal fishing

Illegal, unreported and unregulated (IUU) fishing occurs on the high seas and in areas within national jurisdiction. It is a key driver of global overfishing, threatens marine ecosystems and is linked to major human rights violations, such as modern slavery, and organised crime. "IUU fishing undermines national and regional efforts to manage fisheries sustainably and conserve marine biodiversity" (FAO, 2022c).

IUU fishing may account for up to 26 million tonnes of fish a year – more than 15 per cent of the world's total, not to mention the tonnes of bycatch it contributes to global fish waste (FAO, 2016). It is estimated that as much as one in every five fish caught comes from IUU fishing (United Nations, 2022). When such fish end up on someone's plate, they are unwitting accomplices in unsustainable, and often criminal practices, that are damaging for the future wellbeing and sustainability of the planet. But you can help change that by going vegan!

Fishing – the source of plastic rubbish

Several million tonnes of mismanaged plastic waste enter the world's oceans from coastal cities and rivers every year. Although most of it accumulates on shorelines and on the seabed close to land, there are several offshore plastic accumulation zones in the world and studies suggest that much of the plastic in them comes from industrial fishing.

The Great Pacific Garbage Patch, for example, is a mass of floating plastic waste, three times the size of France, located halfway between Hawaii and California. The plastic gathers where ocean currents converge, forming a 1.6 million square kilometre 'rubbish patch' that includes an estimated 1.8 trillion pieces of plastic. A study published in *Scientific Reports* found that up to 86 per cent of the plastic items were abandoned, lost or discarded by fishing vessels (Lebreton *et al.* 2022). Fishing nets and ropes made up a large proportion of the waste but other objects used in fishing were found, such as floats, buoys, crates, buckets, baskets, containers, drums, jerry cans, fish boxes and eel traps. This debris is sometimes mistaken for food by turtles and other animals and can trap wildlife.

Cleaning up the oceans requires us to first know where the plastic pollution comes from – this research leaves us in no doubt – industrial fishing is a major problem.

EVERY POUND OF FARMED
SALMON REQUIRES THREE
POUNDS OF WILD-CAUGHT FISH

Fish farming is not the solution

There are two types of commercial fish production – capture fishing (wild caught species from oceans, seas, rivers and lakes) and aquaculture (the farming of fish under controlled salt and freshwater conditions – basically underwater factory farms). Aquaculture has grown massively; from 1960 until 2015, it increased 50-fold to over 100 million tonnes per year. Aquaculture has now surpassed capture fishing as its share in total production reached 57 per cent (FAO, 2022c).

Fish farming is often touted as the answer to overfishing but in reality it exacerbates the problem through its reliance on wild-caught fish to feed farmed fish. That's right, large numbers of wild fish are being caught from the sea to produce fishmeal – to feed farmed fish!

For example, on average, every pound of farmed salmon consumes three pounds of wild-caught fish (Gross, 2008). In 2020, around 20 million tonnes of fish were reduced to fishmeal and fish oil (FAO, 2022c), which is still considered the most nutritious and digestible ingredient for farmed fish feeds. Fish are fed other ingredients in feed too such as wheat, rice, rapeseed oil, palm oil, and soya – which links farmed fish directly to deforestation.

Fish farms transmit disease and foul coastal waters with a long list of organic and chemical contaminants, including faeces that choke marine life with excess nutrients, surplus additive-laden feed, antibiotics, pesticides, toxic paints and disinfectants (Gross, 2008). The FAO says: "Aquaculture growth has often occurred at the expense of the environment" (FAO, 2022c).

Viva! has investigated fish farms and found alarming scenes at Scottish salmon farms where invasions of flesh-eating parasitic sea lice were devouring the captive fish alive. On 'high welfare' fish farms supplying luxury food retailers, our investigators saw rainbow trout severely overcrowded and suffering from stress, abrasive injury and predation. Further harm is done when sea lice breach the confines of fish farms and infect wild salmon populations.

Read more about Viva!'s fish investigations here: viva.org.uk/animals/aquatic-wildlife/fish

Subsidies must stop

"From an ecological perspective we cannot afford to destroy the deep-sea. From an economic perspective, deep-sea fisheries cannot occur without government subsidies. And the bottom line is that current deep fisheries are not sustainable" says Rashid Sumaila, professor of ocean and fisheries economics at the University of British Columbia in Canada (SeaWeb, 2007).

"90% of fish stocks are used up – fisheries subsidies must stop" was the title of an article written by Mukhisa Kituyi, secretary-general of the United Nations Conference on Trade and Development (UNCTAD) and Peter Thomson, United Nations special envoy for the ocean. They described how nearly 90 per cent of the world's marine fish stocks are now fully exploited, overexploited or depleted and say that there is no doubt that fisheries subsidies play a big role. Without them, they say, we could slow the overexploitation of fish stocks, deal with the overcapacity of fishing fleets and tackle the scourge of IUU fishing (UNCTAD, 2018).

"90% OF FISH STOCKS ARE USED UP — FISHERIES SUBSIDIES MUST STOP"

The United Nations Climate Change Conference (COP21) – which led to the Paris Agreement – highlighted the urgency of reversing overexploitation and pollution to restore aquatic ecosystems (FAO, 2016). Since then, COP28 has been and gone and government action is still sadly lacking.

GREAT FISH WILL GO THE WAY OF THE DINOSAURS

In 2006, marine ecologist Professor Boris Worm warned that a business-as-usual approach seriously threatens global food security, coastal water quality and ecosystem stability, affecting current and future generations for years to come (Worm et al., 2006). More recently, he said: "Without a doubt, global fisheries are in for a hard landing if nothing changes" (Worm, 2016). Nothing has!

Consider a world where tuna, sharks and swordfish are mere memories says Ransom Myers: "We are in massive denial and continue to bicker over the last shrinking numbers of survivors, employing satellites and sensors to catch the last fish left. We have to understand how close to extinction some of these populations really are. And we must act now, before they have reached the point of no return. I want there to be hammerhead sharks and bluefin tuna around when my five-year-old son grows up. If present fishing levels persist, these great fish will go the way of the dinosaurs" (SeaWeb, 2003).

Without a dramatic shift in the business-as-usual course for marine management, research suggests the oceans will endure a mass extinction that will rank among the major extinctions (Payne *et al.*, 2016). The most effective way to stop the destruction of marine life is to leave the fish alone and go vegan.

Photo © Simon Ager

Food waste and world hunger

The FAO estimates that a third of all food produced for humans is wasted, which amounts to over a billion tonnes a year (FAO, 2011). The World Health Organisation says around 10 per cent of the world's population, more than 800 million people, went hungry in 2021 and more than three billion can't afford a healthy diet (WHO, 2021). In the UK, as the cost-of-living crisis grips, seven million people – one in 10 – are struggling to afford to eat (FareShare, 2022). Precious resources are being wasted producing food that will never be eaten and will use up even more resources being disposed of and, as it rots in landfill, produces methane and further contributes to climate change.

Food production is a major contributor to climate change, producing 35 per cent of global emissions (Xu *et al.*, 2021). This means over 10 per cent of global greenhouse gas emissions may come from food that ends up in the bin! The emissions from wasted food is estimated to be similar to that from all road transport (FAO, 2015). If that wasn't shocking enough, if food waste were a country, it would be the third biggest emitter in the world after the US and China (UNEP, 2021a).

If you throw a burger or some chicken in the bin, you are also throwing away all the grain and water that was used to produce that

30% CEREALS
In industrialised countries, consumers throw away 286 million tonnes of cereal products.

20% DAIRY PRODUCTS
In Europe alone, 29 million tonnes of dairy products are lost or wasted every year.

35% FISH AND SEAFOOD
8% of fish caught globally is thrown back into the sea. In most cases they are dead, dying or badly injured.

45% FRUITS AND VEGETABLES
Almost half of all the fruit and vegetables produced are wasted.

20% MEAT
Of the 263 million tonnes of meat produced globally, over 20% is lost or wasted.

20% OILSEEDS AND PULSES
Every year, 22% of the global production of oilseeds and pulses is lost or wasted.

45% ROOTS AND TUBERS
In North America and Oceania alone, 5,814,000 tonnes of roots and tubers are wasted at the consumption stage alone.

Figure 11. Food losses and waste for each food group per year
Source: FAO, 2015a.

meat, as well as the energy and costs of staff, transport, slaughter, retail and storage, plus the wildlife killed or displaced by expanding pasture or animal feed croplands. Unsustainable and resource-intensive food production is bad enough, without producing food just to be thrown away.

As shown in Figure 11, an astonishing fifth of meat produced globally is lost or wasted – that's equivalent to 75 million cows (Global Panel, 2018). In Europe, 29 million tonnes of dairy products are wasted every year. Around eight per cent of all fish caught are thrown back into the sea – mostly dead, dying or badly injured (FAO, 2015). More are wasted after being sold and cooked. This amounts to an extraordinary number of living creatures being raised, transported and killed for absolutely nothing.

In the UK, the average family throws away over £700 worth of food every year – enough to make eight meals a week. British charity WRAP says that the emissions from the 4.5 million tonnes of food thrown away in the UK are equivalent to those generated by one in every five cars on our roads (WRAP, 2021).

When you waste food, you waste water too. The FAO estimates that the global blue water footprint of food waste (ie the consumption of surface and groundwater resources) is around 250 cubic kilometres – equivalent to the volume of water that flows through the Volga River – the largest river in Europe (FAO 2013). This is the amount of water it would take to fill 100 million Olympic-sized swimming pools!

Although less meat and dairy may be wasted compared to cereals or vegetables, animal-based foods are the biggest contributor to emissions from food waste (Costello *et al.*, 2016). With increasing levels of food insecurity for many people around the world, addressing food waste is a critical issue to creating low-impact, healthy and resilient food systems (UNEP, 2021a).

If we are going to develop sustainable food systems, we must stop wasting food. This will help improve food security and combat the climate crisis (Kummu *et al.*, 2012). Saving food means you'll be contributing to a better legacy for generations to come. A vegan diet could play an important role in preserving environmental resources and in reducing hunger and malnutrition in poorer nations (Baroni *et al.*, 2007). Going vegan and avoiding food waste? Now that's a legacy to be proud of.

Time for action

Over the last few decades, scientists have been warning governments that climate change is already happening; global average temperatures have increased, oceans have warmed, snow and ice have melted and sea levels have risen. We are seeing extreme weather events with increasing frequency around the world.

Paris – emission impossible?

In 2015, governments around the world joined together in the Paris Agreement to try and keep global heating to less than 2°C above pre-industrial levels, ideally below 1.5°C. This is the threshold above which some of the impacts we are already seeing today could tip over from bad to outright terrifying. These critical 'tipping points' would transform life as we know it. Global temperatures have now risen by around 1.1°C and we are edging towards 1.5°C (IPCC, 2021).

Time is running out!

The UN Intergovernmental Panel on Climate Change (IPCC) produces reports every year or so assessing the situation and warning us what the future might hold if no action is taken. The IPCC's report in 2018 was seen by many as the '12 years to save the world' report. In it, leading climate scientists warned there was only a dozen years for global heating to be kept below 1.5°C, beyond which, they warned, even half a degree will significantly worsen the risks of drought, floods, extreme heat and poverty for hundreds of millions of people (IPCC, 2018).

A code red for humanity

The IPCC's 2021 report warned that both the 1.5°C and 2°C limits of the Paris Agreement will be breached unless there are rapid and severe cuts in emissions. UN Secretary General António Guterres described the report as "a code red for humanity". They warned that we may be nearing abrupt changes and tipping points – such as rapid Antarctic ice sheet melt and forest dieback (IPCC, 2021).

Despite the promises and commitments, we are not on track to meet our climate targets – there remains a huge gap between what governments promised to do and what they have actually done. Their promises are little more than hot air and the role of animal agriculture continues to be largely ignored.

Some positive steps have been made in reducing our reliance on fossil fuels and developing technologies for producing renewable energy, but much more action is needed. It doesn't help that the Government over-claim on their achievements by ignoring our oversees emissions. A tactic also often used by the meat and dairy industries to understate emissions associated with livestock farming. We live in a global economy and rely heavily on imports to meet our demands and those of animal agriculture (eg animal feeds crops grown overseas). Many of the goods we buy are made in countries like China and India, so despite the Government bathing in glory, we are not on track to meet our climate targets.

71

"Without addressing food production, tackling biodiversity loss and limiting temperature rise to 1.5°C will be impossible – even if all fossil fuel emissions ceased immediately" (Harwatt *et al.*, 2022).

GOVERNMENTS AND BUSINESS LEADERS ARE LYING

The UN Environment Programme's *Emissions Gap Report 2022: The Closing Window – Climate crisis calls for rapid transformation of societies* says that the international community is falling far short of the Paris goals, with no credible pathway to 1.5°C in place. Only an urgent system-wide transformation, they say, can avoid climate disaster (UNEP, 2022). Scientists at Chatham House agree: "Current global biodiversity and climate change mitigation plans up to 2030 lack detail and suitable levels of ambition" (Harwatt *et al.*, 2022). They say: "The immediate focus must be on reducing the burden of animal agriculture. However, current ambitions to decrease farm-level impacts alone are insufficient, and action is also needed to reduce production of animal-sourced foods (Harwatt *et al.*, 2022).

In 2022, António Guterres warned: "We are on a fast track to climate disaster. Major cities under water. Unprecedented heatwaves. Terrifying storms. Widespread water shortages. The extinction of a million species of plants and animals. This is not fiction or exaggeration.

"We are on a pathway to global warming of more than double the 1.5°C limit agreed in Paris. Some government and business leaders are saying one thing but doing another. Simply put, they are lying. And the results will be catastrophic. This is a climate emergency" (United Nations, 2022a).

Myth-busting

There is a wealth of misinformation and tall tales about food and its impacts on the environment. From grass-fed beef to soya, avocados and almonds – here, we set the record straight.

Is grass-fed beef environmentally friendly?

No, grass-fed beef requires even more land than grain-fed cows and there simply isn't room to produce grass-fed beef for all meat-eaters. Also, grass-fed beef produces up to four times more methane. The pro-meat lobby argue that grazing cattle helps combat global heating by stimulating soil to take up more carbon from the atmosphere. However, a report by the Food Climate Research Network at the University of Oxford found that cattle fed on grass release more greenhouse gas emissions than they are able to offset through soil carbon sequestration. This means that grass-fed beef is "in no way a climate solution" says the lead author of the report. Returning grassland to native woodland would be the ultimate way to sequester carbon and meet our climate goals.

Is organic meat more environmentally friendly?

No. Although organic systems use slightly less energy than conventional systems, organic systems require more land, have a higher eutrophication potential (which, among other things, leads to aquatic dead zones), and emit similar greenhouse gas emissions to conventional systems. And of course, although organically farmed animals may have better feed and some access to outdoors, Viva!'s investigations have shown that they often endure horrific living conditions and, of course, are still sent to slaughter and killed at a fraction of their natural lifespan. Going vegan, however, offers large environmental benefits.

Don't you need animal manure to grow food?

No. An increasing number of growers across the UK have proved this. Tolhurst Organic Farm in south Oxfordshire is a veganic farm – no artificial fertilisers and no animal products. They employ a seven-year rotation to keep the soil healthy including two years of green manure crops (legumes, such as lucerne/alfalfa and various clovers) and a further over-wintering of green manure. The 17 acres supply 400 families for 51 weeks of the year with 75 per cent of their vegetable needs. The Artisan Grower in Aberdeenshire, also veganic, amends their soil throughout the season with alfalfa, minerals from rocks and seaweed! Bridgefoot Organic Co-op, also in Aberdeenshire, use a humus builder made from red clover, chicory, cox foot and ryegrass to enrich their 7.5 acres that supply a range of fruit and vegetables to 200 customers a week, year-round. These are just a few examples of stockfree farms – there will be more.

Is it better to 'eat local'?

Buying locally sourced meat and dairy is not a solution to the climate crisis as transportation (food miles) makes up a very small amount of the total carbon footprint of food and what you eat is far more important than where your food travelled from – and plant foods win hands down. According to the research group Our World in Data from the University of Oxford, eating local is one of the most misguided pieces of advice.

Soya

Soya is a great food for humans – rich in nutrients including B vitamins, fibre, potassium, magnesium and high-quality protein. It's also used widely in animal feed and around 80 per cent of the world's soya is used for beef, chicken, egg and dairy production (WWF, 2020). Soya expansion is a major driver of deforestation as rainforests are being torn down to make way for grazing land and soya, grown for animal feed. If you want to save the rainforests, eat less meat and dairy. Much of the soya used for soya milk is grown in Europe or Canada. If you want a sustainable breakfast, ditch the bacon and eggs and reach for the tempeh rashers and scrambled tofu!

Almonds and avocados

Almonds and avocados are the two plant foods constantly blamed for using too much water and having to travel from the Americas, which makes them less environmentally friendly – or does it? It's true that avocados and  almonds need more water than some other plants but there's more to it than that. They grow on trees which store carbon and release oxygen, helping to keep the atmosphere healthy. Both foods are transported by boat, not air as some people think, and that is less polluting. Although transport only makes up a small part of the carbon footprint of food, if you wanted to eat food grown a little closer to home, both almonds and avocados are grown in Spain.

Quinoa and chia seeds

These traditional South and Central American foods have been consumed by local populations for millennia because they are nutritious and easy to cultivate. But is importing them sustainable? We tend to use only small amounts of either so one pack goes a long way and they're also transported by sea rather than air. But things have moved on and both quinoa and chia seeds are now grown in the UK by the pioneering company Hodmedod's. So, you can get local, fully sustainable quinoa and chia seeds!

Viva! Farming was launched to help farmers transition away from using animals in agriculture in order to establish a more sustainable food system. The aim is to provide the necessary information and support to farmers who take pride in the fact they feed the nation but want to do so in a more sustainable and just way. See vivafarming.org.uk to find out more about sustainable cruelty-free farming.

Conclusion

Animal agriculture lies at the heart of all the environmental problems we are facing; from global heating, deforestation and the vandalising of oceans, to the pollution of the air we breathe. Human activity has caused a sixth mass extinction and we have no idea what the consequences will be. It's like driving a car along a cliff edge while wearing a blindfold. The stark warnings of climate scientists from all corners of the globe are clear: there is still time to turn things around – but only just. Urgent and drastic action is required now if we are to avert disaster.

The IPCC has issued repeated warnings about the impending, devastating consequences of unmitigated climate change. It is not just extreme weather events, rising sea levels, floods and storm surges we need to be concerned about (as if that wasn't enough!), but also political unrest, mass migrations and conflict. The future of our planet is in jeopardy but our leaders are fiddling while Rome burns!

The Government's refusal to name and shame animal agriculture as the major driver of the climate crisis and other environmental catastrophes that afflict the planet, makes it necessary for groups like Viva! to act. We draw attention to the devastating effects that eating meat and dairy has on our planet; if we don't do it, who will?

Changing the way you eat is the single most effective action you can take as an individual to lower your impact on the environment. Scientists say the widespread adoption of a vegan diet could reduce food-related emissions by 50-80 per cent. If we are to stand any chance of achieving zero emissions – as governments claim to be our goal – changing our diets must be pushed right to the top of the agenda. There is a clear path to achieving this, by changing our food systems and rewilding grazing land.

Ordinary people are recognising the severity of the problem, but there is no clear guidance from governments and diet continues to be a universal blind spot, even among some environmental campaigning groups. It is entirely possible for the UK to achieve net-zero emissions, but it will require a concerted effort. Currently, there is a distinct lack of political will for change.

Action is long overdue, but you can empower yourself through the food choices you make. Indeed, this is a vital part of the solution for confronting the biggest threat the planet has ever faced. Yes, we need politicians to listen to the science and do their job by dropping the rhetoric and setting effective targets. But you don't have to wait for them to get on board before you begin making impactful changes. You can make a difference right now by going vegan – for the future of all life on Earth! Your dietary choices can either be part of the problem or part of the solution in addressing the climate crisis.

Now, better than ever, we understand what needs to be done. We understand this needs to be done over the next decade if we want to avoid the worst of climate change. That is both a hopeful but also an urgent message. Go vegan for the future of the planet!

Sign up to Viva!'s V7 programmes to receive daily emails with mouth-watering meal plans, nutritional advice and health information: viva.org.uk/v7

References

Bailey R, Froggatt A and Wellesley L. 2014. Livestock – Climate Change's Forgotten Sector. Chatham House. https://www.chathamhouse.org/publication/livestock-climate-change-forgotten-sector-global-public-opinion-meat-and-dairy

Baroni L, Cenci L, Tettamanti M et al. 2007. Evaluating the environmental impact of various dietary patterns combined with different food production systems. *European Journal of Clinical Nutrition*. 61 (2) 279-286.

Bar-On YM, Phillips R and Milo R. 2018. The biomass distribution on Earth. *Proceedings of the National Academy of Sciences*. 115 (25) 6506-6511.

Bauer SE, K Tsigaridis and R Miller. 2016. Significant atmospheric aerosol pollution caused by world food cultivation. *Geophysical Research Letters*. 43, 5394-5400.

Benton T, Bieg C, Harwatt H et al. 2021. Food system impacts on biodiversity loss. Three levers for food system transformation in support of nature. https://www.chathamhouse.org/2021/02/food-system-impacts-biodiversity-loss

BMC. 2017. Global methane emissions from agriculture are larger than reported, according to new estimates. www.biomedcentral.com/about/press-centre/science-press-releases/29-09-17

Boyce DG, Lewis MR and Worm B. 2010. Global phytoplankton decline over the past century. *Nature*. 466 (7306) 591-596.

Brinkmann K, Noromiarilanto F, Ratovonamana RY et al. 2014. Deforestation processes in southwestern Madagascar over the past 40 years: what can we learn from settlement characteristics? *Agriculture, Ecosystems and Environment*. 195, 231-243.

Bryngelsson D, Wirsenius S, Hedenus F et al. 2016. How can the EU climate targets be met? A combined analysis of technological and demand-side changes in food and agriculture. *Food Policy*. 59, 152-164.

Bureau of Investigative Journalism. 2021. Reign of fire: blazes surge on 'protected' Amazon land under Bolsonaro. https://www.thebureauinvestigates.com/stories/2021-07-31/reign-of-fire-blazes-surge-on-protected-amazon-land-under-bolsonaro

Bureau of Investigative Journalism. 2021a. British chicken driving deforestation in Brazil's "second Amazon". Soya used to feed UK livestock linked to industrial-scale destruction of vital tropical woodland. https://www.thebureauinvestigates.com/stories/2020-11-25/british-chicken-driving-deforestation-in-brazil

Carbon Brief. 2021. Met Office: Atmospheric CO2 now hitting 50% higher than pre-industrial levels. https://www.carbonbrief.org/met-office-atmospheric-co2-now-hitting-50-higher-than-pre-industrial-levels/

Carlsson-Kanyama A and González AD. 2009. Potential contributions of food consumption patterns to climate change. *American Journal of Clinical Nutrition*. 89 (5) 1704S-1709S.

Carrington D. 2018. Avoiding meat and dairy is 'single biggest way' to reduce your impact on Earth. https://www.theguardian.com/environment/2018/may/31/avoiding-meat-and-dairy-is-single-biggest-way-to-reduce-your-impact-on-earth

Cassidy ES, West PC, Gerber JS and Foley JA 2013. Redefining agricultural yields: from tonnes to people nourished per hectare. *Environmental Research Letters*. 8, 3.

Chase MJ, Schlossberg S, Griffin CR *et al.* 2016. Continent-wide survey reveals massive decline in African savannah elephants. *PeerJ*. 4, e2354.

Costello C, Ovando D, Clavelle T *et al.* 2016. Global fishery prospects under contrasting management regimes. *Proceedings of the National Academy of Sciences USA*. 113 (18) 5125-5129.

Davies R, Cripps S, Nickson A *et al.* 2009. Defining and estimating global marine fisheries bycatch. *Marine Policy*. 33, 661-672.

Danson T and D'Orso M. 2011. Oceana: our endangered oceans and what we can do to save them. New York: Rodale.

Defra. 2011. Mapping and understanding the UK palm oil supply chain. A research report completed for the Department for Environment, Food and Rural Affairs. HMSO.

Dummett C and Blundell A. 2021. Illicit harvest, complicit goods – The state of illegal deforestation for agriculture. Forest Trends. https://www.forest-trends.org/publications/illicit-harvest-complicit-goods/

Eisen MB and Brown PO. 2022. Rapid global phaseout of animal agriculture has the potential to stabilize greenhouse gas levels for 30 years and offset 68 percent of CO_2 emissions this century. *PLoS Climate*. 1 (2) e0000010.

EKOenergy. 2020. Climate change: causes and consequences. https://www.ekoenergy.org/extras/climate-change/

Erb KH, Lauk C, Kastner T *et al.* 2016. Exploring the biophysical option space for feeding the world without deforestation. *Nature Communications*. 7, 11382.

Estrada A, Garber PA and Chaudhary A. 2019. Expanding global commodities trade and consumption place the world's primates at risk of extinction. *PeerJ*. 7:e7068

European Environment Agency. 2021. Abundance and distribution of selected species in Europe. https://www.eea.europa.eu/ims/abundance-and-distribution-of-selected

FAO. 2006. *Livestock's Long Shadow*. www.fao.org/docrep/010/a0701e/a0701e00.HTM

FAO. 2011. Global food losses and food waste – extent, causes and prevention. Rome.

FAO. 2013. Food wastage footprint: impacts on natural resources (Summary Report). www.fao.org/docrep/018/i3347e/i3347e.pdf

FAO. 2015. Food loss and waste facts. http://www.fao.org/3/i4807e/i4807e.pdf

FAO. 2015a. Infographic: Food loss and waste facts https://www.fao.org/save-food/news-and-multimedia/news/news-details/fr/c/320086/

FAO. 2016. The state of world fisheries and aquaculture 2016. www.fao.org/3/a-i5555e.pdf

FAO and IMWI. 2017. Water pollution from agriculture: a global review. https://www.fao.org/3/i7754e/i7754e.pdf

FAO. 2018. Why bees matter – the importance of bees and other pollinators for food and agriculture https://www.fao.org/3/i9527en/i9527en.pdf

FAO. 2020. Global Forest Resources Assessment 2020: Main report. Rome. https://doi.org/10.4060/ca9825en

FAO. 2020a. The state of world fisheries and aquaculture 2020. Sustainability in action. Rome. https://doi.org/10.4060/ca9229en

FAO. 2021. AQUASTAT – FAO's global information system on water and agriculture. http://www.fao.org/aquastat/en/overview/methodology/water-use

FAO. 2022. Global Livestock Environmental Assessment Model (GLEAM). https://www.fao.org/gleam/dashboard-old/en/

FAO. 2022a. Water Scarcity – One of the greatest challenges of our time. https://www.fao.org/fao-stories/article/en/c/1185405/

FAO. 2022b. The state of the world's forests 2022. https://www.fao.org/3/CB9360EN/online/src/html/executive-summary.html

FAO. 2022c. The state of world fisheries and aquaculture, towards blue transformation. https://www.fao.org/3/cc0461en/cc0461en.pdf

FAO and UNEP. 2020. The State of the World's Forests 2020. Forests, biodiversity and people. Rome. https://www.fao.org/3/ca8642en/ca8642en.pdf

FAOSTAT. 2022. https://www.fao.org/faostat

FareShare. 2022. Food waste and hunger in the UK. https://fareshare.org.uk/what-we-do/hunger-food-waste

Filbee-Dexter K. 2020. Ocean forests hold unique solutions to our current environmental crisis. *One Earth*. 2 (5) 398-401.

Forest Declaration Assessment Partners. 2022. Forest Declaration Assessment: Are we on track for 2030? Climate Focus (coordinator and editor). www.forestdeclaration.org

Fuller R, Landrigan PJ, Balakrishnan K *et al*. 2022. Pollution and health: a progress update. *Lancet Planet Health*. 6 (6) e535-e547.

Gerbens-Leenes PW, Mekonnen MM and Hoekstra AY. 2013. The water footprint of poultry, pork and beef: A comparative study in different countries and production systems. *Water Resources and Industry*. Vols 1-2, 25-36.

Gerber PJ, Vellinga T, Opio C *et al*. 2010. Greenhouse gas emissions from the dairy sector, a life cycle assessment. Food and Agriculture Organisation of the United Nations, Animal Production and Health Division, Rome, Italy. www.fao.org/3/k7930e/k7930e00.pdf

Gerber PJ, Steinfeld H, Henderson B *et al*. 2013. *Tackling climate change through livestock: A global assessment of emissions and mitigation opportunities. Food and Agriculture Organisation of the United Nations.* FAO, Rome, Italy. http://www.fao.org/3/a-i3437e.pdf

Global Panel. 2018. Preventing nutrient loss and waste across the food system: Policy actions for high-quality diets. Policy Brief No. 12. London, UK: Global Panel on Agriculture and Food Systems for Nutrition. http://www.fao.org/news/story/en/item/1165001/icode/

Goudarzi S. 2007. Caution: Don't eat fish as old as your grandmother. https://www.livescience.com/4383-caution-eat-fish-grandmother.html

GOV.UK. 2022. United Kingdom methane memorandum. https://www.gov.uk/government/publications/united-kingdom-methane-memorandum/united-kingdom-methane-memorandum

Gregg WW, Rousseaux CS and Franz BA. 2017. Global trends in ocean phytoplankton: a new assessment using revised ocean colour data. *Remote Sensing Letters*. 8 (12) 1102-1111.

Gross L. 2008. Can Farmed and Wild Salmon Coexist? *PLoS Biology*. 6 (2) e46.

Harwatt H and Hayek M. 2019. Eating away at climate change with negative emissions. https://animal.law.harvard.edu/wp-content/uploads/Eating-Away-at-Climate-Change-with-Negative-Emissions%E2%80%93%E2%80%93Harwatt-Hayek.pdf

Harwatt H, Wetterberg K, Giritharan A *et al*. 2022. Aligning food systems with climate and biodiversity targets – assessing the suitability of policy action over the next decade. https://www.chathamhouse.org/sites/default/files/2022-10/2022-10-14-food-systems-climate-biodiversity-harwatt-et-al.pdf

Hayhow DB, Eaton MA, Stanbury AJ *et al*. 2019. *The State of Nature 2019*. The State of Nature partnership.

Heinke J, Lannerstad M, Gerten D *et al*. 2020. Water use in global livestock production opportunities and constraints for increasing water productivity. *Water Resources Research*. 56, 12, 2019-26995.

Hilmi N, Chami R, Sutherland MD *et al*. 2021. The role of blue carbon in climate change mitigation and carbon stock conservation. *Frontiers in Climate*. 3, 710546.

Howard J. 2016. 'Mad Max' is a lot scarier when you realize that's where we could be headed. https://www.huffingtonpost.co.uk/entry/mad-max-fury-road-climate-change_n_56d4669de4b0871f60ec0926

Hribar C and Schultz M. 2010. Understanding concentrated animal feeding operations and their impact on communities. Bowling Green, OH: National Association of Local Boards of Health. https://www.cdc.gov/nceh/ehs/docs/understanding_cafos_nalboh.pdf

IATP. 2022. Emissions impossible: Methane edition. https://www.iatp.org/emissions-impossible-methane-edition

IPBES. 2019. UN report: nature's dangerous decline 'unprecedented'; species extinction rates 'accelerating'. https://www.un.org/sustainabledevelopment/blog/2019/05/nature-decline-unprecedented-report/

IPCC. 2014. IPCC. 2014. Climate Change 2014: Synthesis report. Contribution of Working Groups I, II and III to the Fifth Assessment Report of the Intergovernmental Panel on Climate Change [Core Writing Team, RK Pachauri and LA Meyer (eds.)]. IPCC, Geneva, Switzerland, 151 pp.

IPCC. 2018. Summary for Policymakers. In: Global warming of 1.5°C. An IPCC special report on the impacts of global warming of 1.5°C above pre-industrial levels and related global greenhouse gas emission pathways, in the context of strengthening the global response to the threat of climate change, sustainable development, and efforts to eradicate poverty. Cambridge University Press, Cambridge, UK and New York, NY, USA, pp. 3-24.

IPCC. 2021. Climate Change 2021: The physical science basis. Contribution of Working Group I to the Sixth Assessment Report of the Intergovernmental Panel on Climate Change. Cambridge University Press, Cambridge, United Kingdom and New York, NY, USA, 2391 pp.

IPCC. 2022. Climate Change 2022: Impacts, adaptation and vulnerability. Contribution of Working Group II to the Sixth Assessment Report of the Intergovernmental Panel on Climate Change. Cambridge University Press. Cambridge University Press, Cambridge, UK and New York, NY, USA, 3056 pp.

IUCN. 2022. The IUCN red list of threatened species. https://www.iucnredlist.org

Jalava M, Kummu M, Porkka M, *et al*. 2014. Diet change – a solution to reduce water use? *Environmental Research Letters*. 9, 074016.

Jaureguiberry P, Titeux N, Wiemers M *et al*. 2022. The direct drivers of recent global anthropogenic biodiversity loss. *Science Advances*. 8 (45) eabm9982.

Jiang Y, Wang G, Liu W *et al*. 2020 Modelled response of South American climate to three decades of deforestation. *Journal of Climate*. 34, 2189-2203.

Kummu M, de Moel H, Porkka M *et al*. 2012. Lost food, wasted resources: global food supply chain losses and their impacts on freshwater, cropland, and fertiliser use. *Science of the Total Environment*. 438, 477-489.

Krupnick M. 2022. Methane emissions from 15 meat and dairy companies rival those of the EU. https://www.theguardian.com/environment/2022/nov/15/methane-emissions-meat-dairy-companies

Lawrence D, Coe M, Walker W *et al*., 2022. The unseen effects of deforestation: Biophysical effects on climate. *Frontiers in Forests and Global Change*. 5, 756,115.

Lebreton L, Royer SJ, Peytavin A *et al*. 2022. Industrialised fishing nations largely contribute to floating plastic pollution in the North Pacific subtropical gyre. *Scientific Reports*. 12, 12666.

Lesschen JP, van den Berg M, Westhoek HJ *et al*. 2011. Greenhouse gas emission profiles of European livestock sectors. *Animal Feed Science and Technology*. 166-167, 16-28.

Li Q, Jia Z, Feng L *et al*. 2018. Dynamics of biomass and carbon sequestration across a chronosequence of Caragana intermedia plantations on alpine sandy land. *Scientific Reports*. 8 (1) 12432.

Lymbery P. 2022. Sixty harvests left: how to reach a nature-friendly future. Bloomsbury Publishing. London.

Machovina B, Feeley KJ and Ripple WJ. 2015. Biodiversity conservation: The key is reducing meat consumption. *Science of the Total Environment*. 536, 419-431.

Mammal Society. 2020. Red list for Britain's mammals. https://www.mammal.org.uk/science-research/red-list/

Marrs RH, Lee H, Blackbird S *et al*. 2020. Release from sheep-grazing appears to put some heart back into upland vegetation: a comparison of nutritional properties of plant species in long-term grazing experiments. *Annals of Applied Biology*. 177, 152-162.

Maxwell SL, Fuller RA, Brooks TM *et al*. 2016. Biodiversity: The ravages of guns, nets and bulldozers. *Nature*. 536 (7615) 143-145.

MCBI. 2007. Marine Conservation Biology News: The last wild hunt: Deep-sea fisheries scrape bottom of the sea. https://mcbi.marine-conservation.org/what/what_pdfs/LastWildHuntPR_FinalFeb14_2007.pdf?ID=150

McMichael AJ, Powles JW, Butler CD and Uauy R.2007. Food, livestock production, energy, climate change, and health. *Lancet*. 370 (9594) 1253-1263.

Mekonnen MM and Hoekstra AY. 2010. The green, blue and grey water footprint of farm animals and animal products. Value of Water Research Report Series No.48, UNESCO-IHE.

Mekonnen, MM and Hoekstra AY. 2012. A global assessment of the water footprint of farm animal products. *Ecosystems*. 15 (3) 401-415.

Met Office. 2022. A milestone in UK climate history. https://www.metoffice.gov.uk/about-us/press-office/news/weather-and-climate/2022/july-heat-review

Mora C, Tittensor DP, Adl S *et al*. 2011. How many species are there on Earth and in the ocean? *PLoS Biology*. 9 (8) e1001127.

Morell V. 2015. Meat-eaters may speed worldwide species extinction, study warns. https://www.science.org/content/article/meat-eaters-may-speed-worldwide-species-extinction-study-warns

Myers RA and Worm B. 2003. Rapid worldwide depletion of predatory fish communities. *Nature*. 423 (6937) 280-283.

NOAA Fisheries. 2019. Fishing Gear: Pelagic Longlines. https://www.fisheries.noaa.gov/national/bycatch/fishing-gear-pelagic-longlines

Payne JL, Bush AM, Heim NA *et al*. 2016. Ecological selectivity of the emerging mass extinction in the oceans. *Science*. 353 (6305) 1284-1286.

Pimm SL, Jenkins CN, Abell R *et al*. 2014. The biodiversity of species and their rates of extinction, distribution, and protection. *Science*. 344 (6187) 1246752.

Platts PJ, Mason SC, Palmer G *et al*. 2019. Habitat availability explains variation in climate-driven range shifts across multiple taxonomic groups. *Scientific Reports*. 9 (1) 15039.

Poore J and Nemecek T. 2018. Reducing food's environmental impacts through producers and consumers. *Science*. 360 (6392) 987-992.

Reid C, Hornigold K, McHenry E *et al*. 2021. State of the UK's Woods and Trees 2021. Woodland Trust.

Roman J, Estes JA, Morissette L *et al*. 2014. Whales as marine ecosystem engineers. *Frontiers in Ecology and the Environment*. 12 (7) 377-385.

Sala E, Mayorga J, Bradley D *et al*. 2021. Protecting the global ocean for biodiversity, food and climate. *Nature*. 592, 397-402.

Sánchez-Bayo F and Wyckhuys KAG. 2019. Worldwide decline of the entomofauna: A review of its drivers. *Biological Conservation*. 232, 8-27.

Sandström V, Valin H, Krisztin T *et al*. 2018. The role of trade in the greenhouse gas footprints of EU diets. *Global Food Security*. 19, 48-55.

Scarborough P, Appleby PN, Mizdrak A, Briggs AD, Travis RC, Bradbury KE and Key TJ. 2014. Dietary greenhouse gas emissions of meat-eaters, fish-eaters, vegetarians and vegans in the UK. *Climate Change*. 125 (2) 179-192.

Schultz AA, Peppard P, Gangnon RE *et al*. 2019. Residential proximity to concentrated animal feeding operations and allergic and respiratory disease. *Environment International*. 130, 104911.

SeaWeb. 2003. Nature cover story – Only 10% of all large fish are left in global ocean. https://www.eurekalert.org/news-releases/805075

SeaWeb. 2007. The last wild hunt: deep-sea fisheries scrape bottom of the sea. ScienceDaily. www.sciencedaily.com/releases/2007/02/070218130829.htm

Spring J and Boadle A. 2021. Brazil's Amazon deforestation surges to 15-year high, undercutting government pledge. https://www.reuters.com/world/americas/brazil-deforestation-data-shows-22-annual-jump-clearing-amazon-2021-11-18/

Springer AM, Estes JA, van Vliet GB *et al*. 2003. Sequential megafaunal collapse in the North Pacific Ocean: an ongoing legacy of industrial whaling? *Proceedings of the National Academy of Sciences USA*. 100 (21) 12,223-12,228.

Strokal M, Ma L, Bai Z *et al*. 2016. Alarming nutrient pollution of Chinese rivers as a result of agricultural transitions. *Environmental Research Letters*. 11 (2) 024014.

Stroud JL. 2019. Soil health pilot study in England: Outcomes from an on-farm earthworm survey. PLoS One. 14 (2) e0203909.

TABLE. 2022. Soy in the UK: What are its uses? https://www.tabledebates.org/blog/soy-uk-what-are-its-uses

Twine R. 2021. Emissions from animal agriculture – 16.5% Is the new minimum figure. *Sustainability*. 13, 6276.

UNCTAD. 2018. 90% of fish stocks are used up – fisheries subsidies must stop. https://unctad.org/news/90-fish-stocks-are-used-fisheries-subsidies-must-stop

Unearthed. 2020. Demand for animal feed is driving the hazardous pesticide industry, data reveals. https://unearthed.greenpeace.org/2020/02/20/meat-soya-animal-feed-pesticides-hazardous/

UNEP. 2004. Cold-Water Coral Reefs UNEP-WCMC, Cambridge. UK. https://ia600303.us.archive.org/2/items/coldwatercoralre04frei/coldwatercoralre04frei.pdf

UNEP. 2021. COVID-19, climate change threaten last refuge of the mountain gorilla. https://www.unep.org/news-and-stories/story/covid-19-climate-change-threaten-last-refuge-mountain-gorilla

UNEP and Climate and Clean Air Coalition. 2021. Global methane assessment: Benefits and costs of mitigating methane emissions. Nairobi: United Nations Environment Programme. https://www.unep.org/resources/report/global-methane-assessment-benefits-and-costs-mitigating-methane-emissions

UNEP. 2021a. UNEP Food Waste Index Report 2021. https://www.unep.org/resources/report/unep-food-waste-index-report-2021

UNEP. 2022. Emissions Gap Report 2022: The closing window – climate crisis calls for rapid transformation of societies. Nairobi. https://www.unep.org/emissions-gap-report-2022

UNESCO. 2017. Facts and figures on marine biodiversity. http://www.unesco.org/new/en/natural-sciences/ioc-oceans/focus-areas/rio-20-ocean/blueprint-for-the-future-we-want/marine-biodiversity/facts-and-figures-on-marine-biodiversity/

UNICEF. 2022. Nearly 600 million children will live in areas with extremely limited water resources by 2040 – UNICEF. https://www.unicef.org/press-releases/nearly-600-million-children-will-live-areas-extremely-limited-water-resources-2040

United Nations. 2022. International Day for the Fight against Illegal, Unreported and Unregulated Fishing 5 June. https://www.un.org/en/observances/end-illegal-fishing-day

United Nations. 2022a. Secretary-General Warns of Climate Emergency, Calling Intergovernmental Panel's Report 'a File of Shame', While Saying Leaders 'Are Lying', Fuelling Flames. https://press.un.org/en/2022/sgsm21228.doc.htm

UN News. 2019. Ensuring the 'lungs of the planet' keep us alive: 5 things you need to know about forests and the UN. https://news.un.org/en/story/2019/05/1038291

van Marle MJE, Field RD, Werf GR *et al*. 2017. Fire and deforestation dynamics in Amazonia (1973-2014). *Global Biogeochemical Cycles*. 31 (1) 24-38.

Vaughan A. 2019. Deforestation in Brazil has rocketed since Bolsonaro became president. www.newscientist.com/article/2210621-deforestation-in-brazil-has-rocketed-since-bolsonaro-became-president/#ixzz5vvN2WZay

Vieno M, Heal MR, Twigg MM et al. 2016. The UK particulate matter air pollution episode of March-April 2014: More than Saharan dust. *Environmental Research Letters*. 11, 4.

Waycott M, Duarte CM, Carruthers TJ et al. 2009. Accelerating loss of seagrasses across the globe threatens coastal ecosystems. *Proceedings of the National Academy of Sciences*. 106 (30) 12377-12381.

Weiskopf SR, Rubenstein MA, Crozier LG et al. 2020. Climate change effects on biodiversity, ecosystems, ecosystem services, and natural resource management in the United States. *Science of the Total Environment*. 733, 137782.

WHO. 2021. UN Report: Global hunger numbers rose to as many as 828 million in 2021. https://www.who.int/news/item/06-07-2022-un-report--global-hunger-numbers-rose-to-as-many-as-828-million-in-2021

Woodland Trust. 2020. Ancient woodland. www.woodlandtrust.org.uk/press-centre/2020/01/thousand-threatened-ancient-woods

World Economic Forum. 2022. Here's how the Earth's forests have changed since the last ice age. https://www.weforum.org/agenda/2022/04/forests-ice-age

World Meteorological Organisation. 2022. The first Red extreme heat warning issued in UK during European heatwave. https://public.wmo.int/en/media/news/first-red-extreme-heat-warning-issued-uk-during-european-heatwave

Worm B, Barbier EB, Beaumont N et al. 2006. Impacts of biodiversity loss on ocean ecosystem services. *Science*. 314 (5800) 787-790.

Worm B. 2016. Averting a global fisheries disaster. *Proceedings of the National Academy of Sciences*. 113 (18) 4895-4897.

WRAP. 2021. Food surplus and waste in the UK – key facts. https://wrap.org.uk/resources/report/food-surplus-and-waste-uk-key-facts

WWA. 2022. High temperatures exacerbated by climate change made 2022 Northern Hemisphere soil moisture droughts more likely. https://www.worldweatherattribution.org/without-human-caused-climate-change-temperatures-of-40c-in-the-uk-would-have-been-extremely-unlikely/

WWA. 2022a. Climate change likely increased extreme monsoon rainfall, flooding highly vulnerable communities in Pakistan. https://www.worldweatherattribution.org/wp-content/uploads/Pakistan-floods-scientific-report.pdf

WWF. 2018. Living planet report 2018: Aiming higher. wwf.panda.org/knowledge_hub/all_publications/living_planet_report_2018/

WWF. 2020. Living Planet report 2020. https://livingplanet.panda.org/en-us/

WWF. 2022. 92% of fish discarded in EU fisheries linked to trawling – WWF study. https://www.wwfmmi.org/plastic/?uNewsID=6393966

Xu X, Sharma P, Shu S et al. 2021. Global greenhouse gas emissions from animal-based foods are twice those of plant-based foods. *Nature Food*. 2, 724-732.